Dreams Unseen

Dreams Unseen

WALTER PIERCE

Copyright © 2021 Walter Pierce.

All rights reserved. No part of this book may be reproduced in any form or by any electronic or mechanical means, including information storage and retrieval systems, without permission in writing from the publisher, except by reviewers, who may quote brief passages in a review.

ISBN: 978-1-63821-638-4 (Paperback Edition)
ISBN: 978-1-63821-639-1 (Hardcover Edition)
ISBN: 978-1-63821-637-7 (E-book Edition)

Some characters and events in this book are fictitious. Any similarity to real persons, living or dead, is coincidental and not intended by the author.

Book Ordering Information

Phone Number: 315 288-7939 ext. 1000 or 347-901-4920
Email: info@globalsummithouse.com
Global Summit House
www.globalsummithouse.com

Printed in the United States of America

CONTENTS

Chapter 1:   The Foreigner 1
Chapter 2:   Step And Shatter 21
Chapter 3:   The Power Transfer 44
Chapter 4:   The Drain 57
Chapter 5:   The Old Warriors 84
Chapter 6:   America 103
Chapter 7:   The Scientists 112
Chapter 8:   The Madman 124
Chapter 9:   The Four 137
Chapter 10: The Assassins 149
Chapter 11: The Red Realm Archers 163
Chapter 12: The Date 176
Chapter 13: The Young Warriors 188
Chapter 14: The Alliance 201
Chapter 15: Broken Chains 214
Chapter 16: The Revenge Of Maubuus 226
Chapter 17: Heart Of The Warriors 246

CHAPTER 1

THE FOREIGNER

The Yellow Realm...

There is a beautiful plain where yellow grass grows on the rolling hills. The hills stretch for miles into the horizon. On a flat area, several warriors stand in a great circle. At the center of that circle is an old man known as Doorway. Doorway is old but his skill at opening doors to other realms is at its best. He -as all the Doorways had been-is the center of the warriors.

Arrow leads the warriors. A man every warrior has great trust in. Arrow was truly a special leader. But then again all the warriors were special. Each was born with a power from their ancestors -a power known as the Shine.

They had protected their people many times and today they would do the same. They stood waiting, staring off into the distance. Straining to see the evil forces that they knew would come...

The Blue Realm (Earth)...

In the Japanese countryside there is a boy named Hideo. He goes to a boring school, lives in a boring area, and has a boring life. But still he manages to have his fun...

He imagines himself doing all kinds of exciting heroic deeds. He imagines himself fighting a great battle against impossible odds and winning. He imagines doing inhuman feats and saving beautiful women. He always ends by imagining himself ready to face a great beast, the thing that scares him the most, a great evil dragon! He goes and stands in front of a cave. He calls out to the dragon in a voice that isn't as mighty as he wishes. The dragon's eyes can be seen in the darkness. It starts to come closer. Fear begins to fill him but he raises his sword to welcome the dragon. The dragon begins to call his name as the ground shakes -just like Hideo.

Dreams Unseen

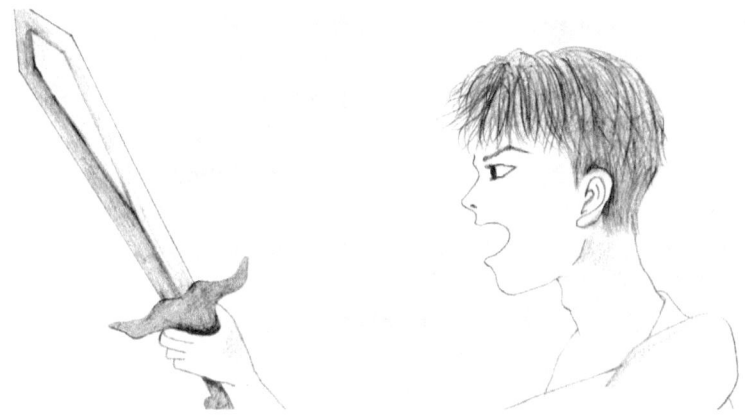

Suddenly, the scene changes and he is sitting in class holding his pencil in the air. All the kids in the class are laughing. Some are calling him names. The teacher has a very angry look on his face. Then the bell rings and all the children leave. Hideo coyly glances at the teacher who motions for Hideo to come to him.

The Yellow Realm...

In the distance dust could be seen rising.

Step: They're coming. It looks like there are a lot of archers.

Arrow: A lot of Archers? Must be some new strategy by Maubuus.

Mist: It looks like we're going to have a lot of bows and arrows to play with when this battle's over!

Step: Gee, I sure hope they use the high quality wood and not the cheap stuff.

Suddenly the sky goes black. All the warriors shine with their powers. For a moment there is silence with the eerie scene. Then there is sheer chaos as fire begins to rain down from the sky. It is centered on Doorway and he is knocked unconscious.

Earth (Early Evening)...

Beside a stream, a lonely young man named Hideo worries about his situation...

Hideo: Everybody teases me. They all think I'm strange. Maybe I am. My parents are going to kill me too. This is the fourth time this week my teacher has caught me daydreaming! He's going to call and tell my parents. They'll make me study forever! I'm tired of this life. I wish I could just fly away like a bird and never come back!!

He begins to daydream about being a bird. But the dream is interrupted. There is a "Wheem" sound as a little ball of yellow light appears and opens into a circle in mid air. This has got to be a dream Hideo thinks as he sits there with his mouth wide open. Looking into the circle he could see a totally different place, a place where there seemed to be multiple fires, bright lights and the sound of battle. He doesn't get to look for long because a figure bounds through the doorway. Hideo would've run but he sees that it is an old man who falls when he comes through the door. The door disappears after a few seconds. Hideo is frightened as he watches the old man try to stand. Hideo cautiously approaches him.

Hideo: Excuse me. Are you okay?

Doorway: Help me, please.

Hideo: Are you okay?

Hideo reaches the old man and reaches down to help him up. The old man lurches up and grabs Hideo. Hideo's eyes grow big with shock. Not only because he is grabbed but also because of the strength of the old man's grip.

Doorway: I am dying. There must be a doorway. By all of the ancestors, I pass my power to you. You are my choice. May all of the ancestors see and bless the choice I've made...

Hideo: What? Let me go!

There is the "Wheem" sound again. Hideo feels that there is a ball of light put into his belly. His body seems to glow for a second.

Doorway: Arrow. Find Arrow. There must be a doorway.

Hideo: What are you talking about?

Doorway: The Red Realm!

The old man says this with all his strength. Again there's the "wheem" sound but this time a tingle goes through Hideo. A red ball of light appears and opens beneath their feet. They fall through the door and exit in mid air. They find themselves a good 200 feet above the ground. Somehow, they quickly reach and hit the ground of a strange planet. The impact separates Doorway and Hideo. As they hit the ground, Hideo hears a double wheem sound as the doorway disappears. Hideo, sore from the fall, looks over and sees that the old man is dead. Hideo also notices that both of them are wet. Hideo feels so confused by all of this. Hideo's head is swimming.

Hideo: Now what am I going to do? How do I get home? And where am I?

Fear fills him as he desperately tries to think of what to do.

Hideo: Help me! Help me! No one's here to hear me! Old man you can't be dead! Get up and help me get back home.

An explosion and a scream interrupt the sounds of the jungle area. Hideo doesn't know whether to run away from or towards the explosion. The noises and the explosions seem to be coming closer so Hideo decides to just hide. Suddenly, a man with a bow and arrow comes into the clearing.

Hideo: Could this be the Arrow person that the old man kept talking about? Maybe he can get me home...

His thoughts are cut short as he sees an arrow of light zip out of the jungle and hit the man. The man is torn apart by the arrow.

Hideo: My God.

Hideo has never seen anything like this. His heart pounds as he shivers in the bushes. Then another man comes into the clearing. He is panting and staggering. Then his eyes see Doorway's dead body so he runs over to the body.

Arrow: It's over. Our people will die...

Hideo: (thinking) They must have been friends. Maybe he is Arrow. He doesn't have a bow or an arrow though. How can I be sure? I think I'd better just try to find my own way home.

Hideo turns and begins to slowly creep away.

Arrow: There must be a Doorway!

The words stop Hideo in his tracks.

Hideo: Those are the words the old man said. He must be Arrow.

Hideo turns back around and slowly creeps out of his hiding place. He cautiously walks toward the man.

Hideo: Excuse me.

Arrow flips around while moving his hands like he's drawing a bow. As he does, there's a "wheem" sound and a bow and arrow of light appear out of nowhere. Aimed directly at Hideo's head.

Hideo: (Raising his arms) Don't shoot! (thinking: oh this was a mistake!)

Arrow: Who are you?!

Hideo: I'm Hideo.

Arrow: What do you want?!

Hideo: I..uh..uh..the old man brought me here. He said find Arrow.

A look of severe distrust covers Arrow's face. But he lets the bow of light disappear.

Arrow: Why?

Hideo: I don't know.

Arrow: What did he say to you?

Hideo: He said the same thing that you said. He said that there must be a doorway.

Arrow: He couldn't have meant you. There couldn't have been enough time to pass the power to you. And you're nothing more than a child. You're not even one of my people.

Hideo: Listen; I don't know what he meant. I was just hoping that you could get me home.

Arrow gives a look that displays how displeased he is with what Hideo has just said. Then he begins to speak as if he never heard him.

Arrow: Definitely King Maubuus will launch an attack on my people now that he knows that they are defenseless. Our first job will be to go back to the people and mobilize whatever kind of fighting force we can.

The strain shows as he talks and breathes heavily.

Hideo: We?? I just want to go home. Please just tell me how to get home.

Arrow: Child, I think you have been chosen to be the Doorway. -There must be a door. King Maubuus will slaughter my people as a whole without you.

Hideo: Your situation sounds really bad. I really would like to help but I'm no warrior.

Arrow: I know. You are a child. But Doorways do not really fight. They transport and protect the warriors. They protect by opening doors in front of objects that are about to hit the warriors. See, your job isn't so dangerous but it is very important.

Arrow used the word "child" like a knife. Hideo could feel the injury with each use.

Hideo: I'm a student not a doorway! I don't even know how to help you.

Arrow: You just don't understand. All you have to do is open the doors, you stupid child! Outsiders are nothing but trouble!

Hideo: No, you don't understand. I can't open the doors. I'm a human!

Arrow's face changes and he seems to calm down a bit.

Arrow: I didn't think there was enough time to pass the power to you. But how did you get here child?

Hideo: I told you. The old man opened a door and we came here.

Arrow: So, you are sure he didn't pass the power to you.

Hideo: I don't think so. He said some strange things and I felt strange.

Arrow: Have you tried to open a door?

Hideo: No.

Arrow: This is important. If he didn't give you the power then we're both trapped here. Concentrate and imagine a yellow light appearing.

Hideo nods… There is complete silence as he combines his concentration with his imagination. Then the silence is broken with a chiming "wheem" sound accompanied by a glorious tingle that goes through his body. Then a spinning ball of light appears in mid air. Hideo stands in awe that he could do something so special. The yellow light was so beautiful that he could only stare at it while his heart pounded from exhaustion and excitement.

Arrow: Are you going to open it or kiss it?

Hideo: What? Oh, I'm sorry.

Arrow: We don't have time for this! Open it!

At that moment, an arrow flies by Hideo's head and many footsteps can be heard approaching. Arrow and Hideo turn and run for cover.

Arrow: More?? How many of these guys came through the red doors. Child, use your door to block the arrows and I'll fire at our attackers.

Arrows fly wildly as several archers reach the clearing. Arrow fires a few arrows of his own then falls to his knees from exhaustion. Everything was happening so fast. This was Hideo's chance to be a real hero just like in his dreams. Everything depended on him.

Hideo: I've got to open that door and maybe I can block those arrows.

It is actually quite easy to open the door. It only takes a brief thought. But the result isn't exactly what Hideo expected. The door opens into the vacuum of outer space! Things begin being sucked into the door from both sides. Trees, dirt, plants, rocks, and Doorway's dead body head for the door. Also, the archers, Hideo and Arrow are pulled towards the door.

Arrow somehow manages to fire a weak arrow towards the door. The Arrow zips through the chaos and somehow it closes the door. But the momentum of the flying objects keeps them moving. So, there is a terrible collision in the area where the door was.

Archer, Arrow, Hideo: Oh, oh...

Everyone that is not unconscious tries to get to his or her feet. Soon the ones standing are involved in a wild fistfight. Hideo tries to be like the hero he dreams of being. He finds out that dreams hit a lot softer than real villains...

Hideo: I am Hideo. Ungh.

As he gets knocked out. Arrow is getting beat up by two archers. The two archers grab and hold both his arms. The third archer begins violently beating Arrow.

Lead Archer: Now you will die! Just like the ones you led at the battle of the fire!

He draws a knife and grimaces as he walks toward Arrow.

Lead Archer: Ha, ha, ha...ungh!

The lead archer falls forward. There behind him is a fist. A fist of light! A somewhat fat man in his mid 40s comes from behind the fist. He has a very angry look in his eyes.

Barrier: Let him go...NOW!

The two archers drop Arrow and run into the jungle. Barrier runs over to Arrow.

Barrier: Let's get out of here! Who knows how many of them came through the red doors!

Arrow: Barrier?...Yes...ungh...br...un..uu..bring the child.

Barrier: Who is he?

Arrow: A problem.

In the world of dreams...

Hideo stands before the same cave he dreamed of in class. He can see the evil eyes of the dragon as before. Hideo turns and runs. He runs into the old Doorway.

Old Doorway: Where are you going?

Hideo: Somewhere safe. -Away from the dragon.

Old Doorway: You can't run away from your fears. They will chase you. They will always haunt you. You must stand up and face your fears.

Hideo: How can I? I am weak.

Old Doorway: There is strength inside of you. You must not run away.

Hideo: How...how can I help your people? I want to help them but I'm afraid and I'm not even one of your people!

Old Doorway: You are not one of our people. Your thinking is different. Hideo, that's the key! With new thinking and a respect for the old ways my people can be saved. But you must not run away!

Hideo: But please show me how. Please help me.

Old Doorway: I already have.

Hideo turns toward the cave. He walks boldly holding a sword.

Hideo: I'm coming to get you!

Dragon: Then I will devour you, child!!

...

Arrow: Child! Child, wake up!

Hideo: Huh...huh.

Arrow: Wake up! It's morning already! I was weak and passed out. Barrier let me sleep. Now, we won't even have time to raise an army from among my people. I estimate that by now King Maubuus has amassed a large army and it's on its way to destroy my people!! Practice your power as much as you can while I try to come up with a plan.

Barrier: What makes you think we have any chance at all against them?

Arrow: Shut up, Barrier! I didn't ask you if you used the blue shield.

Arrow's words confuse Hideo but Barrier seems to understand. His expression turns decidedly glum.

Arrow: You stinking coward! Our situation is truly bad! I only have a child and a coward to rely on!

That word "child" was really starting to anger Hideo.

Hideo: I'm not a child! I can fight!

Arrow: Fight?! You just don't understand our ways child!! Barrier, help the child practice his powers while I think.

Arrow walks off into the jungle. Barrier begins to help Hideo practice using his power.

Barrier: Well, let's start by opening and closing one door.

Hideo: Ok.

After about fifteen minutes of practice.

Hideo: What's the blue shield?

Barrier: My barriers have different colors of light. Their use depends on the color. Blue is my strongest barrier.

Hideo: Why was Arrow so angry when he asked you about it?

Barrier: It's my strongest but I can only use it to protect myself. And I also can't fight while using the blue shield.

Hideo: oh.

Barrier: Everything happened so fast at the battle of the fire - the battle where all the warriors died. Maubuus' men were all around us. Fire and smoke was everywhere. My friends were dying and attacks were coming from everywhere. So, I put up the blue shield until I heard the doors opening. I ran through a red one.

Hideo: So, other warriors could've survived too.

Barrier: It's possible. Now let's try to open two doors at the same time. Concentrate on seeing two green balls of light appearing.

Hideo: Ok.

Hideo grimaces.

Hideo: I'm trying but I can't.

Barrier: It's ok. Try to imagine only one green door.

There's a "wheem" and a green ball of light appears.

Barrier: Now try to imagine a second door.

There's another "wheem" and a second green door appears.

Hideo: Why did Arrow get angry when I said that I would fight?

Barrier: Your power isn't an attack power. It's defensive. It has always been the job of the Doorway to transport and protect the other warriors. This tradition goes back to the very first Doorway.

Hideo: I am certainly not fast enough with the doors to protect either of you. I probably couldn't even protect myself.

Barrier: This is a big problem. I don't know why Arrow wants you at the battle we are going to have. Maybe it is because the situation is so desperate or maybe because he is such a traditional thinker. The old saying goes, "There must be a Doorway."

Hideo: That is quite a popular saying with you guys.

Barrier: That saying also goes back to the time of the first Doorway. He prophesied that when the Doorway leaves all the warriors will die.

Hideo: Do you believe the prophecy?

Barrier: I don't believe it and I don't disbelieve it. All I know is that without the warriors my people will die at the hands of King Maubuus.

Out of the corner of his eye, Hideo sees a figure...Arrow has returned.

Arrow: Let's go.

Barrier: You've got a plan?

Hideo: Three against an army. What's the plan?

Arrow: You simply do what I say. We'll follow the old ways and the ancestors will smile on us.

Hideo: What kind of plan is that?!

Arrow: Quiet child and listen. We'll put ourselves between the army and the land of our people. Hideo will stay in the middle and ward off any projectiles that come toward us or towards him. Barrier will assist in this while they are at a distance. I will fire my arrows and take out as many as I can. Once some get too close we'll retreat through an open door. We'll put a safe distance between them and us and then we'll start to fight again.

Hideo: That plan sounds like suicide. How many arrows can you shoot before you're physically exhausted? My ability to use these doors doesn't measure up to the necessary skill or speed to make your plan work. They'll overwhelm us. They'll get through the doors before I can close them -even if I can open them!

Arrow: Don't question me! That is the plan, child! Follow it!

Hideo: I won't! I'll go home! You're not my boss.

Arrow: How? Do you know how to get home?

Hideo: No.

Arrow: If I told you would you open a door for us to go and battle Maubuus' men?

Hideo: Sure.

Hideo was a bit surprised with the question. He could hear defeat in Arrow's voice. Even Arrow didn't believe in his plan.

Arrow: You said that you were human. That means that you are from the blue realm. Think of your home and open a blue door.

Hideo: Thank you.

Arrow: Now open a yellow door for us so that we can go fight. Think of a field and of this drawing.

Arrow begins to draw on the ground.

Hideo: You two will die.

Arrow: Maybe. But it is better to fight than run away child. You can run away and dream about being the hero that you know you'll never be.

Hideo doesn't say a word as he opens a yellow door.

Arrow: (Looking through the door) There is a large marching army in tight formation in the distance. Child, open the door closer to them.

Hideo closes the first door and opens a door closer to the army. Barrier steps through the door. Arrow also steps through the door. He stops and looks back.

Arrow: You can run away but you will always be haunted…

Arrow turns and the door closes.

Hideo: …by your deaths.

Hideo turns and opens a blue door. Sure enough it leads to home.

Hideo: What can I do anyway? I'm not even supposed to fight just transport. It's their way. I know that I'm not good enough to protect them so I've done my part.

He continues to talk to himself as he enters the blue door. He continues to try to convince himself that he was right to leave. He fights a battle more hopeless than the warriors.

The Yellow Realm...

Two warriors face a thousand.

Barrier: Well, this is it my friend.

Arrow: We lived and died well. Let's go.

It's a strange feeling knowing that you're going to be dead soon. Arrow motions with his hands and a bow of light appears with the "wheem" sound. Arrow looks at Barrier and then fires. The arrow seems to almost move in slow motion -but much too fast to be avoided! It hits and kills one of Maubuus' men. He screams out as he dies and everything seems to stop. There is silence. Then there are a thousand screams as Maubuus' men CHARGE!

Arrow picks up the pace of his firing. Barrier begins blocking the weapons fired at the two. After about 20 arrows you could see the strain on Arrow's face. The overwhelming horde was getting closer. That's when Barrier's shine completely disappears.

Arrow: Wh..what are you doing?

Barrier: My heart! I'm too old. My chest...

Barrier turns and makes a stumbling retreat. The fierce cries of Maubuus' men fill the air as they get closer and closer. Arrow turns to help Barrier run. He tries to hold Barrier while running but Barrier is too heavy and too weak. Finally, Barrier falls to the ground.

Barrier: R...r...run Arrow. Run!

Arrow: I can't leave you.

Barrier: You're our people's last hope.

Arrow: There is no more hope. The prophecy has come true. Doorway is dead. No Doorway means that all the warriors will die.

An arrow flies out from the approaching horde of warriors. It strikes Arrow in the shoulder. Everything seems blurry and then everything goes dark. He doesn't see that a red door is opening on the ground in front of the charging army. The charging army starts falling into the door. Hideo strains to make the door open as wide as possible. Some soldiers try to turn and run but they crash into the other oncoming soldiers. As soldiers continue to fall, the door continues to open wider. The loud rabbles' cry fades as the last of Maubuus' men make the journey to the red realm.

…Much Later,

Three figures sit silently thinking of the events of the past two days. The new way of thinking, the use of the doorway power offensively had never been done before. None of the enemy warriors had expected it and that's why it worked.

Hideo: I've never felt so tired in my life.

Barrier: Using your power is like using any other part of your body. Using your muscles causes exhaustion and so does using your power.

Arrow: That was a great idea you had.

Hideo: A Doorway not fighting is the way of your people. But I am not one of your people. My thinking is different.

Arrow: Nevertheless, I doubt that it'll ever work again. Maubuus' men know to watch out for that trick now.

Barrier: It doesn't matter because Maubuus can't put together such a large fighting force anymore.

Arrow: That's true.

Barrier: Could this actually be the end of Maubuus' attacks?

Arrow: Maubuus always has tricks up his sleeve. -Like at the battle of the Fire. The things that happened there were unnatural. Yet, we saw none of these tricks at this battle and none of the power that defeated us. Why?

Barrier: Stop being so serious! We just defeated about 80% of Maubuus' army! We took away his ability to attack our people! We avenged the death of so many of our friends!...

With the realization of the deaths of their friends the mood changes.

Hideo: They died because they wanted to protect your people. Their souls are somewhere smiling because we've won.

Arrow: (smiling) Yes. Yes they are...Doorway.

This was the first time that Arrow had called him anything other than child. And for some reason it felt so good.

CHAPTER 2

STEP AND SHATTER

Maubuus' Castle

The Hideous beast, Maubuus, sits on his throne surrounded by beautiful women serving him.

Woman 1: Oh, Maubuus who is greater than you?

Woman 2: You are king of all! Your mighty armies crush all!

Maubuus smiles. Just then he notices one of his soldiers walk in.

Messenger: Sir, I ...h...have bad news. Your army has been defeated.

Maubuus: WHAT!!!

Messenger: One of the soldiers survived. He is badly injured.

Blue Realm Earth

Hideo's mother and father are talking to him.

Father: Why can't you be serious about life! Do you want to get kicked out of school? I'm tired of getting calls from your school telling me that you're not paying attention in class! Hideo, you are 16 years old. It's time for you to grow up.

Mother: And where have you been?

Hideo doesn't answer.

Father: Answer your mother!

Hideo: I..I..

Mother: You've been gone for two days! We were so worried.

Father: No responsibility! No respect! Go to your room and go to bed! You better not be late for school tomorrow!

Yellow Realm...

Two lone figures sit barbecuing a deer over a fire on a vast open yellow plain.

Barrier: We buried so many of our friends today, Arrow.

Arrow: They are still alive in our hearts and in the blood of our people.

Barrier: Did you count the dead of our people?

Arrow: Yes, there were 10 missing.

Barrier: So more could've escaped through the doors.

Arrow: Some of the bodies were very badly burned. The missing 10 may be no more than uncounted ashes.

Maubuus' Castle Dungeon

Two bloodied warriors are chained to the walls.

Step: Are you conscious, shatter?

Shatter: Yes.

Step: Can you shine?

Shatter: If that is a joke your famous humor isn't working... Why don't they just kill us? Why do they constantly torture us to near death and then leave?

Step: I don't know but I noticed they have been collecting our blood.

Shatter: What?! Oh, Step!

She begins and then falls unconscious.

Blue Realm

Next morning...

Hideo's alarm clock goes off.

Hideo: I have to get up now. I promised to transport Arrow and Barrier to their people this morning. And I also can't be late for school.

Hideo hurriedly dresses. His mother sees him, as he is about to leave.

Mother: You are going to school very early this morning.

Hideo: Yes. I..uh..thought about what you and father said and decided to get to school early and study.

Hideo rushes out the door. His mother is a little astonished. As he heads out of sight, his mother smiles.

Mother: Maybe there is hope for you my little Hideo.

Maubuus' Dungeon

Shatter awakens...

Step: Good morning Shatter.

Shatter: Oh, is it time for our regular beating yet?

Step: Almost.

Shatter: Oh, Step I can't take it any more! I'm so scared.

Step: I don't mean to scare you more but I still owe you a kiss for saving my life.

Shatter: Yep, that's scarier than Sinder Forest.

Step: Hey...

Shatter: I don't think you'll ever get a chance to give it... I can't take another beating.

The guard walks in holding his whip. Attached to his waist is a set of keys.

Guard: Are you ready for another whipping?!

Shatter: If I had that whip I'd show you a whipping.

The guard angrily storms toward Shatter and slaps her.

Step: Shatter!! Keep your hands off her!

Step spits in the guard's face. The guard turns toward Step and draws his hand to slap Step. Step flinches and instinctively moves his hand to his face and forms the hypnotic eye. The guard backs up and drops his hands. His eyes glaze over and he stares blankly.

Shatter: What do we do now? That's only going to last a few seconds and when he comes to we're really going to get beat!

Step: The keys! Can you shine Shatter!

Shatter: Maybe a little.

Shatter strains. The effort shows on her face. Then, in her hand appears a sword of light.

Step: Use the sword to get the keys.

Shatter: I...I can't! I'm not strong enough to lift the sword!

Step: Maybe...

Step begins to grimace as he shines with the usual wheem sound. When he shines a square of pure light appears floating in mid air under the sword. He continues to move it up -lifting the sword. The sword lifts the keys off the guard's belt. The keys slide down the sword into Shatter's hand. Utterly exhausted they look at each other and smile.

Step: Looks like I'm going to get to kiss you again after all.

On the yellow field a doorway opens up and young Hideo steps through. He isn't greeted though. Arrow and Barrier are staring off at a dust cloud coming.

Arrow: It's an army!

Arrow grimaces and a bow of pure light appears.

Barrier: It's coming from the direction of our people. Could another army have attacked our people?

Arrow: If they did they're going to pay! Hideo! Get us a better vantage point of this army!

Hideo opens a doorway leading to a hill much closer to the army. The three look closer. It appears to be a rag tag group carrying rocks and clubs. The leader is carrying a sword –a sword of pure light!

Arrow: It's sword. Open a door directly in front of the group.

Hideo: OK.

Hideo opens a door in front of the army. The leader of the army runs to Arrow and they hug. The rabble army begins to cheer and shout.

Sword: You're alive!

Barrier: What happened to you?

Sword: During the battle of the fire a yellow door opened and I went through. It led to an area near our people. So I decided to prepare the people for an attack. I put together an army as quickly as possible.

Arrow: Very good thinking. Come and rest a bit. We need to talk about what happened at the battle of the fire. Hideo open a door for our people to go back home.

Hideo: How do I know where to open the door to?

Arrow: You should be able to feel where the people want to go and open a door to there!

Hideo: Hunh?

Arrow: Empathy...Just do it!

Hideo opens a yellow door. And someone in the crowd says, "No, not there." Hideo tries again but is again wrong. Soon there is a raucous cacophony of sounds -sounds of doors opening and closing. And of complaints, "No, not there!"

Arrow turns to Barrier, who obviously has something on his mind.

Barrier: It just doesn't seem to make sense.

Arrow: Yes, Maubuus had the perfect chance to destroy our people when he defeated us. But the people were not attacked.

Barrier: And what exactly happened at the battle of the fire? Maubuus had enough power to overwhelm us at the first battle but didn't use it against us the second time.

Sword: I can't answer those questions. I can only tell you what I remember...

Maubuus' Castle Again

Maubuus and a doctor are standing near a man with only one leg and one arm.

Doctor: He used his one leg and one arm to pull himself back to the castle.

Maubuus: My warriors were defeated! How did my army get beaten?

Doctor: He told me that Doorway opened a door to the red realm and sent your army there. He said that Arrow shot him before the door opened. He was left for dead!

Maubuus: My army! Sent to another realm?! A Doorway actually fighting?

The messenger again slips in.

Messenger: I...uh...have bad news. The prisoners have escaped.

Maubuus: WHAT?!! Come here!

The messenger comes. Maubuus grabs his head and crushes it. Then he begins to eat the head.

Doctor: Finding another messenger will not be an easy thing.

Elsewhere...

Sword: I was standing next to Shatter when everything went dark. Then there seemed to just be fire everywhere.

Sword's eyes look confused as he looks to Arrow.

Having finally found the right place. Hideo joins the three warriors.

Hideo: Where did the fire come from?

Sword: I don't know... Then the next thing I knew Maubuus' men were all around us. My sister and me stood back-to-back fighting Maubuus' warriors. There was smoke and fire everywhere. We heard the sounds of battle in the background but we only paid attention to the ones we were fighting. But then we heard the voice of Step. He was falling from the sky. My sister ran trying to get to where he was. I saw an archer grab Shatter from behind. I threw my sword and stabbed him in the back. Shatter continued to run. She dived and caught Step in the air. She balled herself up and rolled when she hit the ground. That's when an archer hit me. Everything was so confused. I clenched my fist and my sword was with me again. I fought but now there were three fighting me. I was so exhausted. That's when doors opened everywhere. I glimpsed at my sister and Step being carried away. One of the archers hit me in the face and I fell through a yellow door. I made my way to our people and I tried to prepare them for an attack. The attack never came. Arrow ...did you find my sister among the dead?

Barrier: No. We didn't find Step either. In total there are about 10 warriors unaccounted for.

Sword: They're still alive! We have to save them!

Hideo: I hate to interrupt but I really have to be going to school now. If I don't then I'm going to be late!

Arrow: You're going to be late!!!

Maubuus' Castle

Shatter: How long can we just stay here? They're bound to find us.

Step: I know but we have to rest. We can barely shine.

Shatter: Step...

Step: Yes, Shatter?

Shatter: Do you think anyone else is alive?

Step: Of course.

Shatter: We were being overwhelmed at the battle of the fire. We didn't stand a chance. I never thought that I would be as afraid as the time I got lost in Sinder Forest when I was a little girl but now I'm...

Her lovely eyes stare at Step. He sees the little girl in the woman he loves and he holds her.

Step: Don't worry darling everything is going to be OK.

Maubuus' Throne Room

The four great wizards of Maubuus stand before him.

Maubuus: I want those two warriors captured immediately!

Augus: As lead wizard, I have served you faithfully Maubuus. You have my word they will be found.

Maubuus: There are only five of you left but so help me I'll have your blood if you don't capture them!!

Augus: The guards are scouring the castle my lord.

Maubuus screams in anger. He grabs one of the women at his throne. He kisses her passionately then he breaks her back and throws her to the castle floor.

Maubuus: Remove this dead body before I become angry!!

Outside Maubuus' Castle

Some distance away stands Hideo, Arrow, Barrier and Sword.

Hideo: Arrow, my parents are really going to be angry! We have to hurry and do this.

Arrow: Don't you understand? This is not a game! We could die here!

Hideo: I know... I'm just... I don't know.

Barrier: Just explain to your parents that you are a warrior now.

Arrow: Warrior?! He is not warrior! He is a Doorway!

Barrier: Explain that you are a doorway.

Hideo: I can't do that! My parents will think I'm crazy! I can see it now. Mom, I missed school because I opened a door to another realm and was fighting the evil king Maubuus. Not alone, of course, beside a fellow that can make a sword appear in his hand, a guy who fires bolts of light, and a guy who projects hardened energy around his body!

Arrow: ENOUGH! I can't think! Hideo go over there and talk. I don't want to hear your voice!

Hideo looks frustrated like he's about to say something but then he walks away a bit and sits on the ground. Barrier follows.

Barrier: So...uh..school is very important to your parents?

Hideo: Oh yeah. You can't imagine! They want me to become an architect.

Barrier: What's an architect?

Hideo: A person who designs buildings.

Barrier: We don't study to make houses. We just join an experienced person and start building.

Hideo: But what about complex buildings where you have to know a bit of math or physics so that the house won't fall.

Barrier: What's physics?

Hideo: You know... science.

Barrier: What's science?

Hideo: Uh... What do you study in your schools?

Barrier: We study history and the sacred traditions and taboos of our ancestors.

Hideo: Sacred traditions and taboos?

Barrier: Yes, like if the wind blows strongly for 4 days in a row then you should plant corn the next day. If a cat crosses your path you should visit your relatives.

Hideo: Those sound like superstitions.

Barrier: Superstitions?

Hideo: Yeah, like your belief that something horrible will happen if the Doorway leaves.

Barrier is silent.

Hideo: What kind of science do you study?

Barrier: What's science?

Hideo feels a little strange as he looks at Barrier's complete confusion.

The Castle

Step: Keep running Shatter!

Shatter: The guards are everywhere.

Step sees a door that seems to be away from everything.

Step: In here Shatter, quickly!

Step tries to open the door but he can't.

Step: It's locked!

Shatter: Let me try.

Shatter begins to shine. There is a wheem sound as a sword of light appears. She shatters the lock with her sword. Then they run inside. Inside they see a lone wizard, Robius. He is standing next to a large machine. The wizard's eyes get big as he looks at the two blood soaked warriors. The next moment there is an amber beast standing there.

Step: We're warriors. Your hollow illusions won't deter us!

The wizard throws a ball of fire that goes through the beast and heads towards Step's voice. Shatter jumps and pushes Step out of the way at the last minute.

Shatter: You talk too much, Step.

Step: Shatter, I'm shocked. You know I'm a man of action -not words.

With those words, Step jumps up and lands on a step of light. He runs through the air. Every step landing on a step of light that appears with the characteristic "wheem" sound. The wizard throws balls of fire but they all miss. Step is just too quick. The last step he lands on is blue. It has a rubbery nature to it. Step bounces off of it and crashes into the wizard. Step gets up and meets the wizard's rising with a punch. The punch sends the wizard into a big container, which tips over. It's a big vat of blood that spatters everywhere.

The wizard falls unconscious. Step turns to Shatter.

Step: Well?...

Shatter: I stand corrected. You're a lot of both.

Step: What kind of room is this? There's blood everywhere. And look at this weird thing. It has a doorframe built into it but it goes nowhere. This is strange.

Shatter: I don't think hiding in here was such a good idea. Let's go somewhere else.

Step: Or better yet, let's just keep looking for a way out of here.

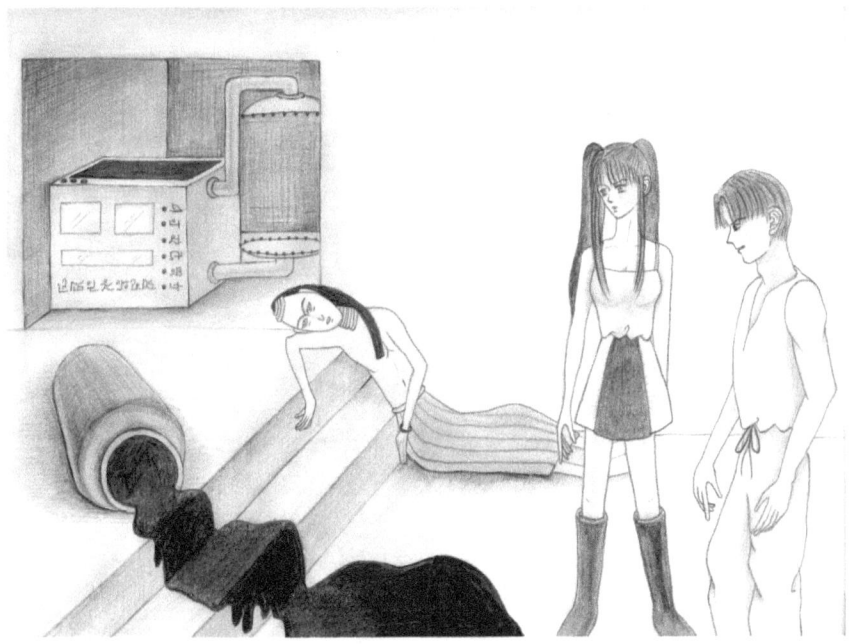

Outside The Castle

Arrow is standing alone staring at the castle. Sword is practicing fighting Barrier. Hideo is standing with his eyes closed. There are 2 balls of green light slowly spinning around him. Hideo is sweating from a combination of the heat of the day and the concentration he is exerting. Unseen by all is a silent figure a little distance away. He simply watches.

Arrow: Warriors!

The warriors come to Arrow's call.

Arrow: Hideo, I need you to open a door.

Hideo: Where?

Arrow: You must feel the correct place to open the door.

Hideo looks puzzled as he mumbles.

Hideo: I feel like opening a door home.

Arrow: You must open a door in the castle.

Everyone stands around looking at Hideo. Hideo looks confused. Arrow begins to look angry.

Hideo: I don't know what to do!

Arrow: Close your eyes and feel the warriors in the castle.

Sword: Maybe they're dead.

Arrow: Shut up Sword! OPEN A DOOR, HIDEO!

There's almost an insanity in Arrow's voice. Hideo immediately opens a door. Arrow immediately runs through the door. Instinctively, Sword and Barrier follow.

Hideo: What am I doing?!

Hideo runs through the door. He comes out in the middle of a throne room -the throne room of Maubuus! He sees the hideous Maubuus sitting on his throne and 4 of Maubuus' wizards standing there. They are wearing blue and gold neck rings. All 4 of them are unusually tall and evil seems to emanate from them. Hideo feels overwhelmed with the sight and stands staring. His imagination never prepared him for this. His trance like stance is broken by Arrow's call to arms.

Arrow: WARRIORS!

Hideo doesn't move, unsure what to do. He watches the fluid like movements of the warriors as they position themselves. Arrow is directly in front of Hideo. To his left and right are Sword and Barrier.

Maubuus: Kill them.

Maubuus is smiling. And finally fear fully hits Hideo.

One of the wizards opens his mouth and snakes fly out. They fly towards Barrier. Barrier puts up his red energy field around himself and begins swinging his fists at the snakes. The snakes swim in air around him flecking their tongues - which are like flecks of mini blue lighting. None of their strikes seem strong enough to penetrate the energy field but Barrier isn't fast enough to hit the snakes.

The second and third wizards open their mouths and 2 swarms of bright pink bugs float out. Arrow fires his arrows at the swarm. His arrows cut swathes through the slow moving bugs. The bugs continue to swarm out. The arrows zip through the swarm and you can hear the tiny slapping sounds of the bugs against the stone floor. The final wizard opens his mouth and a humming sound comes out. It has fluidity that encapsulates Sword. Sword seems to be moving very slowly. It seems to be pushing him backwards. He's fighting against the stream trying to get away.

Hideo: What should I do?

Hideo just watches, as does Maubuus.

Elsewhere in the castle, a group of Maubuus' men run through the castle. Three run into a room where they see a young woman with her back against the wall.

Guard: Now we've got you!

Those are the last words that he says as a rather large stone table falls out of the air onto his head. The other two guards look up to see Step standing on a square step of light waving. As the second guard looks up, he hears the third guard scream. He looks down to see a sword of pure light sticking through the third guard. That's when everything goes dark, as Step jumps onto the guard and his head hits the stone floor.

Shatter: We've made too much noise! Other guards are coming.

Step: Well, let's be going!

They run out of the room and head down a hallway. They immediately turn around and start going in the apposite direction. Behind them, a stream of soldiers follows. Step and Shatter turn and run down a very narrow hallway. Too late do they realize that the hallway dead-ends.

Shatter: Uh Oh! Now we're in for it!

Step: Don't worry. Follow me.

He takes Shatter's hand and runs straight at the line of guards. Just as the lead guard is ready to strike a Step of light appears as Step steps into the air. With every step that Step takes, a step of light appears. Shatter follows as they run over the heads of the guards. The steps disappear quickly after Shatter steps off of them. They move too quickly for the guards in the front and in the middle of the line. But guards at the back have time to see them coming. One of the guards jumps up and grabs Step's leg. Step falls into the group.

Shatter dives into the group, knocking it backwards. She's the first one up. She holds up her sword and shouts.

Shatter: Shatter!

The sword breaks like glass into 5 yellow shards. The shards seem to knowingly hit the 5 guards blocking their path. The guards yell in pain as Step and Shatter streak by them!

Back with Maubuus, Hideo opens door beneath the feet of one of the wizards but the wizard just floats until Hideo closes the door.

Maubuus: young Doorway, we know your tricks. Your warriors are making no headway against my wizards. Soon your warriors will tire and their powers will wane! Look at how savagely they fight even through they have no hope. I can almost feel their hatred!! HA HA HA

Maubuus' horrible laugh echoes in the throne room. Hideo looks around at the warriors. Arrow is wearily running trying to escape the pink bugs that ever float near him. Arrow is also trying to hit the wizards with his arrows but the bugs keep floating in his way. Barrier and Sword are still deadlocked with the wizards they are fighting. Hideo tries to open another door under one of the wizard's feet but again the wizard begins to float.

Hideo: If the warriors become too tired their powers will fade. We're going to lose!

Just then another group of guards run into the throne room. And Hideo realizes that things just got a lot worse.

Hideo: Now we're going to lose faster! Maybe I can open a door under the guards! But they're not mindless they know the trick I used before. They're not mindless! But insects basically are! Maybe...

Hideo concentrates as hard as he can. His efforts pay off as a double "wheem" sound occurs. Two yellow balls of light appear. One in front of the wizards that are creating the pink bugs and the other in front of the six guards who have just come in. Hideo opens the doors. One of the doors is directly in front of the wizards' mouths so the pink bugs go into the door. They emerge out of the other door in front of the 6 guards. The six guards swing their weapons in the air wildly trying to stop the bugs. There are too many of the bugs and they begin stinging the guards. Injecting a fluorescent pink liquid into their victims. The wizards realize what is happening and stop concentrating. It's too late for the guards though. It's also too late for the wizard attacking Sword, as an arrow of pure light rips through him. Sword charges Maubuus. Then he stops and throws his sword at the two wizards that were fighting Arrow. The wizard blocks the sword. The sword disappears and reappears in Sword's hand just in time to block a bolt of lighting thrown by the other wizard. The wizard fighting Barrier stops concentrating and runs away. He runs down a hall and straight into Step and Shatter. Step and Shatter prepare to fight but he just keeps running. Step and Shatter give each other a puzzled look and keep running still just ahead of the pursuing soldiers. They run into the throne room. The last two wizards run to Maubuus. Maubuus rises.

Arrow: Give us our people!

Shatter: Looking for us?

Sword: Shatter!

Sword sees the battered shape that his sister, Shatter, is in.

Sword: You die Maubuus!

Sword again charges Maubuus. Sword throws his sword at Maubuus. Maubuus tries to catch it but it's gone just before it reaches him. The next moment Sword is in front of Maubuus with the sword. Sword swings but Maubuus moves and grabs Sword. He picks Sword up and slams him on the stone. Sword bounces and stops moving. Arrow fires an arrow but it doesn't really harm Maubuus. The soldiers enter the room. Shatter runs to Sword. The wizards converge on her and Sword. Maubuus goes towards the other warriors. The soldiers come towards the warriors too.

Hideo: We're surrounded!

Arrow: We've got what we wanted. Let's go!

Barrier: Shatter and Sword!

The two wizards converge on Shatter with their daggers drawn. Maubuus is between the rest of the warriors and the wizards.

Arrow: Open a door Hideo. I'll get Shatter and Sword.

Maubuus: You'll have to go through me.

Shatter: I'll protect you, brother.

Sword: Oh...

Hideo: Arrow, I'll open a door under them.

Arrow fires at Maubuus but there is no effect. Shatter fights the two wizards. Step and Barrier are trying to hold off the soldiers while Hideo holds open a door. Hideo decides to open a second door under Sword and Shatter. When he does he only gets Sword since Shatter is moving. Barrier has a large barrier of energy keeping the soldiers at bay.

Barrier: I can't keep this up.

Hideo: I've got Sword. Come on everybody.

Maubuus slaps down Arrow. Knocking him over by Hideo. Shatter runs toward Hideo but Maubuus blocks her.

Shatter: Escape while you can!

Maubuus grabs her and crushes her body. Shatter's sword turns black as Maubuus drops her. The wizards and Maubuus begin to move toward Hideo and the battered bodies of Arrow and Sword. Then things get even worse as Barrier can no longer hold up his barrier. Hideo immediately opens an escape door again but all of the warriors won't make it. That's when Shatter's last word is heard.

Shatter: Shatter!

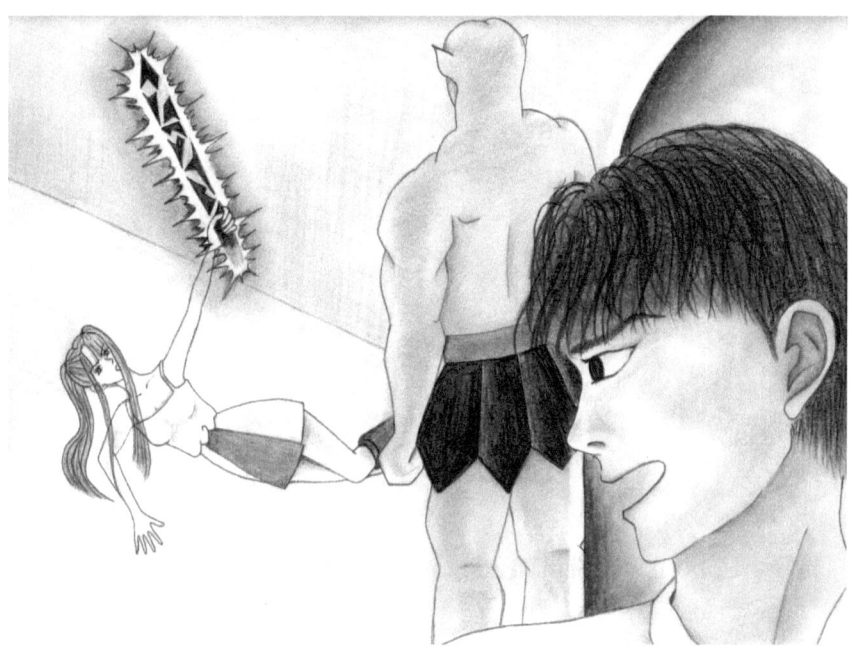

Her sword shatters. Black is the death color of Shatter's power. The sword breaks into 7 shards. 2 hit the wizards and five hit Maubuus. A black inky color spreads over the wizards' bodies and they fall dead. Maubuus staggers backwards. Barrier lifts Arrow and Step lifts Sword through the door Hideo has opened. Shatter bought just enough time. She sweetly smiles at Hideo as she dies. Hideo is the last through the door. Hideo goes through the door and closes it.

CHAPTER 3

THE POWER TRANSFER

The warriors emerge still inside the castle.

Barrier: Where are we?

Step: We're still in the castle. I know this room. Shatter and I came here.

Hideo: I'll open another yellow door to try to get us out of this castle.

Arrow groggily watches the events. Barrier's eye catches the vat of blood.

Barrier: My God! That's blood! Why is there a big vat of blood sitting there?

Hideo glances over as he concentrates to open a door. The blood shocks him but what really hits Hideo is that there is a machine sitting beside the vat.

Hideo: How can that be?

Barrier: What?

Hideo: That. That's a machine! And it looks very complex too.

Step: I've never seen anything like it!

Hideo: It doesn't seem to belong here. Something strange is going on.

Arrow: It could be a weapon! We need to take it. Step, guard the door. Hideo, do you know what that is?

Hideo: I'll take a look.

Hideo looks at the strange rectangular opening in the machine. The opening is about six feet tall and two feet wide. It has a silver look to it but when Hideo touches it he knows that it is made of composite materials -maybe plastic.

Hideo: This is impossible. How?

Arrow: What kind of weapon is it?

Hideo doesn't answer. He continues to run his hand along the machine.

Barrier: Does this have something to do with how we were defeated at the fire?

Sword: Oh,....

Hideo comes to a squat rectangular section of the machine. On here he notices touch pad controls and a cryptic writing system.

Hideo: I can't read the writing. Can you Barrier?

Barrier looks.

Barrier: I have never seen this kind of writing. It is beyond me.

Arrow: Open a door back to our people. We'll try to take the ... maasheen with us.

Hideo tests the weight of the machine and finds that it is unbelievably light. He could almost lift it himself.

Hideo: These two peoples have no technology but this looks more advanced than things in Japan.

Arrow: Hideo, open a door.

Step: We're in trouble. Guards are coming.

Sword: My sister. Where is my sister?

Arrow: Get him through the... Hideo, open a door!

Hideo is trying to imagine how such a piece of technology could have gotten to this backward place.

Hideo: Sorry.

Hideo opens a yellow door back to the plain where the battle of the fire had happened. After everyone comes through the doorway, Arrow scans the area. A look of sheer irritation comes on his face.

Arrow: The wrong place again!!

Hideo: Sorry. I'm still not so good at this.

Arrow: We'll perform the power transfer ritual when we return to our people. So Hideo, open a door.

Again Hideo opens a door. This time he opens a door to the correct place. The warriors' people gather around the yellow door and watch as the warriors come out. The crowd is very large about 4 - 5 thousand people. Hideo doesn't notice so much because his mind is on school and his parents.

Barrier: Are you daydreaming again?

Hideo: In school I used to daydream about being a great warrior. Now I'm daydreaming about school!

Barrier: Arrow has ordered that the power transfer ritual begin in 3 hours. Come walk with me.

Hideo: OK... What exactly is the power transfer ritual?

Barrier: Usually, before Doorways die or before they become too old they pass their power on through the ritual.

Hideo: The old Doorway didn't perform some ritual to give me his power.

Barrier: There's no ritual necessary. It's just tradition.

Hideo: So, just more time is being wasted!

Barrier: Arrow believes in the old ways. This tradition shows respect for God and our ancestors.

Hideo: ... a waste of time. Is this how all the warriors transfer their powers?

Barrier: No, only Doorways transfer their power. We are all born with our power. It usually starts to show itself around the onset of the teenage years.

Hideo: All of your people have some kind of power?

Barrier: No, only some.

Hideo: Why do some have power and others do not?

Barrier: We do not know. It is a blessing that comes to some.

Hideo: Whom will I be transferring my power to?

Barrier: A very special young man named Ramethi. He has been training many years to be a Doorway. He will do well. He is the one that was chosen to be the next Doorway.

Barrier points at a rather skinny young man, who is not too much older than Hideo.

Hideo: He doesn't look special in any way. How was he chosen?

Barrier: When he was younger, it was noticed that empathy was strong in him.

Hideo: Why is that important?

Barrier: Because of the nature of the Doorway's position among the warriors. Doorways protect and transport the warriors. Protection includes opening a door when a warrior needs it.

Hideo: Yeah?

Barrier: Doorways should be able to FEEL when a warrior needs a door opened. You can't do that but it's what Arrow expects. This gets him very angry.

Hideo: Oh...

Maubuus' Castle, 2 hours later...

Maubuus' last two wizards, Robius and Milstar, stand chanting over Maubuus.

Robius and Milstar: Owa Owa Monta owa. Owa Owa Manta owa...

Maubuus: I am tired of this. Go away.

Robius: Oh, Maubuus the black light of the shard grows in you. It will kill you.

Maubuus: I am Maubuus! Do you doubt my strength! Do you think that I could not kill you?

Maubuus grabs him by the neck. He takes fingernail and carves an X on Robius' forehead.

Maubuus: I will thrust a sword through this point in your skull if you anger me again. Now go!

Robius and Milstar hurry away.

A messenger enters as the two wizards hurry out.

Messenger: Oh, great Maubuus. I have a dire message to deliver to you. I pray that you spare my life when you hear the sheer import of the message. Please remember that I...

Maubuus: Deliver the message.

Messenger: ... The Doorway Machine is gone. Stolen by the warriors. So, now we can't get the archers that Doorway sent to the Red Realm back. Please don't kill me.

Maubuus rises. The blackness of the shard in his belly has grown. It spreads towards his chest.

Maubuus: I will kill all the warriors!

Elsewhere...

The lone figure that had been silently watching everything stands before a council, reporting. His name is Jethri.

Jethri: His name is Hideo. He is from the Blue Realm.

Councilman 1: Ah, then this could possibly be the explanation that we've been waiting for. He could be the key.

Jethri: Shall I capture him or kill him?

Councilman 1: Neither. We don't want to trigger what we are trying to avoid.

Jethri: It must be him. The timing of his arrival is too perfect. All the facts point to him being the one.

Councilman 1: There will be no rash reactions. We shall wait for a while and continue to watch. The date is still a ways off.

Councilman 2: I agree. At the rate we are going we'll have enough time to take another look before the date.

Jethri: That's cutting things too close! According to all the projections the rate of energizing crosses the falling threshold of needed energy with less than a week left!

Councilman 2: Caution is the correct path.

Jethri: Caution would be to stop all this now by killing Hideo.

Councilman 3: I do not agree with the council. I feel as Jethri does. Hideo should be killed. But I am outvoted so I will abide by the will of the council. Jethri, you are to gather more evidence.

Jethri: Yes sir. I will.

The City of the Warriors...

The Evening is clear and cool. The yellow grass sways in the breeze. There is a crowd of people with a long wide aisle down the center. Everyone in the crowd is focused on the young man walking down the aisle. He is not of their people but he is a part of their most sacred ritual - the transfer of the power of the Doorways.

All his life he's wanted an adventure but now he doesn't care. He just wants to get this over with. There are so many people staring at him. He's going to have so much trouble at home with his parents and with school. He just wants this over with.

At the end of the aisle stand the warriors with their full shine. Arrow and Sword stand to one side. Sword is being supported by crutches made of tree limbs. Arrow is a bit bruised but seems fine. On the other side is Barrier and Step. Barrier is completely focused on the ritual while Step is recounting the life he had with Shatter.

Hideo makes it to the end of the aisle. There is a ghostly white glow from warriors. It's quite mesmerizing. It makes Hideo forget all his worries and focus on the event. Hideo feels himself begin to glow. From nowhere it seems a priest appears. He's dressed in a golden silk. Beside him comes Ramethi. The priest is mumbling words over the Ramethi's head. Ramethi is the only one not glowing. Hideo can't understand the words that are being said. The tone of the words seem to be growing in volume. Hideo can't understand but pictures begin to flash in his mind. He sees pictures of fire. He feels animals standing behind him. He turns around and sees a group of dogs. A curious feeling overcomes him as he looks at the dogs.

Hideo: Why are they here?

Then Hideo sees their eyes. He feels an intelligence there. He looks into their eyes and realizes that are intelligent beings. They are like men. When that thought enters his head somehow there are people standing there instead of dogs. They don't speak but Hideo feels words. Their eyes seem to speak. Words are there but Hideo can't quite understand them.

Hideo: What are you saying?

Then Hideo hears clearly,

Priest: Doorway.

Hideo: Huh.

Priest: Give me your hand.

Hideo reaches out his hand. The priest holds it over Ramethi's head.

Priest: Let the doors flow away -flow to Ramethi.

Dizzily Hideo feels the lighted orbs flow out of his body. It's like waves of water flowing through his body. Then it feels like his body is engulfed in waves of water. The orbs of light are spinning around Hideo. The beautiful colors silently soothe the evening. The amazement of the crowd seems to be part of the air.

Priest: Do you give these doors to Ramethi?

Hideo: ...Ye...Yes...Yes!

Suddenly the sky becomes dark. Rain bursts from the sky. Thunder booms and lightning flashes fiercely. The crowd disperses and runs for shelter. Their cries of shock fill the darkness, as the rabble gets hysterical.

Dreams Unseen

Hideo: Is this part of the ceremony?

The priest is just standing there looking confused and stunned. Barrier wraps his arm around Hideo and quickly leads him to a little house.

Hideo: What happened?

Barrier: I don't know.

Hideo: I still can open doors. I can feel it.

Just then Arrow, Sword, and the priest come in. Arrow is helping Sword along.

Arrow: We'll have to do the transfer again!

Priest: No. We won't.

Arrow: What are you talking about?

Priest: We are not going to do the ceremony again. The ritual was rejected by the ancestors.

Arrow: So, Hideo will be Doorway! Arg!

Arrow storms over to the door and stares out.

Hideo: Well, I don't want to be this Doorway!

Arrow ignores the challenge.

Sword: Looks like you don't have a choice.

Hideo looks down.

Priest: What did you see?

Hideo: What? I'm not looking at anything.

Priest: No. What did you see at the ceremony? I saw your eyes. I know you saw something.

Hideo: Yes, I did. I imagined the strangest thing. I saw these dogs that were really people. They were standing behind me. And they kept saying...uh...uh "no, the chains will be broken." At least I think that's what they said.

Everyone is silent and looks confused except the priest.

Priest: This is confirmation that Hideo must remain the Doorway. The people stood behind you. This is a symbol for ancestors. They said to you "no." They were obviously against the ritual. They then caused the rain to stop the ritual.

Sword: What about the chains?

Priest: Chains are made of links. It symbolized our links to them. Our links would be harmed or even broken if we continued with the ritual.

Hideo: Why?

Priest: I don't question their will.

Hideo: Oh..no...I better be getting home now.

Arrow: We have no need for you for now. You may go but check back in with us.

Hideo is a little stunned because he wasn't asking for permission. He almost vocalizes it as he glances in Arrow's direction. Arrow still has his back to Hideo. Hideo effortlessly opens a blue door home. Before he goes through he nods farewell to Barrier and Sword. He looks over to Arrow's direction and pauses for a moment. It's not Arrow that catches his eye but a spot outside a window a few yards away from Arrow out in the rain. It almost seems like there is a small spot not being rained on. But Hideo shrugs off his feeling and steps through the door. The day is over!

...A few yards away, in the spot Hideo glanced at, stands Jethri.

Jethri: Amazing. Absolutely amazing.

CHAPTER 4

THE DRAIN

Hideo's home

Home wasn't quite what Hideo expected.

Hideo: I'm home.

Mother: Hello Hideo. How was school?

Hideo: Uh...the same as always. Where's father?

Mother: He's sleep. It's pretty late you know.

Hideo: I know. I'm sorry to come home so late.

Mother: Do you want to tell me where you were?

Hideo: Mother...I can't.

Hideo's mother doesn't say anything else. He can see the worried look on her face. But he also knows that he can't do anything to relieve her. So, he turns and heads for his room. Being a hero wasn't what Hideo had imagined. In his dreams he always knew what to do. The scenarios that he had built in his head had become quite elaborate but he would always know what to do. If he didn't he could always just do things over.

Hideo: What am I going to do? I'm no hero. I didn't know what to do when I was in Maubuus' Castle. And what about my time away from school and having to keep this secret from my parents? Oh, I don't know what to do! Is my life always going to be like this? I wish that I had never met the old man, Doorway. What am I going to do at school tomorrow?

Hideo worries and worries till he falls asleep.

Yellow Realm...

It was late and all the warriors were asleep except one, Arrow. He's alone in a small building. The building which holds the Door Machine.

Arrow: I wonder if this strange thing was the weapon used to overwhelm us at the fire? It is too big and bulky to be a good swinging weapon. Maybe it is some great magic weapon. But the priests do not recognize it. Maybe it is some lifeless beast Maubuus slew.

Arrow runs his hand over the top of machine, completely baffled. Inadvertently he hits a switch that activates the machine. Lights come on and a whirring sound is heard. Arrow lurches back like a cat and a bow and arrow appear by the time his footing is regained. He is prepared to fight as he makes his familiar call.

Arrow: WARRIORS!!

Despite the sounds that the machine is making, it is coldly silent in Arrow's world as he emotionlessly stares at the machine. Some people have gathered by the door of the little building where the machine is. Step pushes his way into the hut. Astonished chatter follows him. But still it doesn't break Arrow's concentration.

Step: Arrow, I'm here.

Barrier makes his way in at this moment.

Barrier: As am I.

Step: It's making noise but that's all.

Barrier approaches the machine with a weak movable green barrier surrounding himself. Step positions himself over the top of the machine.

Arrow: What are you?!

The machine doesn't say anything. Barrier is now close enough to touch it. He lets his barrier down and touches the machine.

Barrier: It's OK. I don't think that it's alive.

He begins touching it more to show that everything is OK. The warriors drop their powers just as a Barrier hits a button that makes the machine begin to hum. The sudden change causes the warriors to immediately begin to shine again. Some of the crowd outside the door begins to flee. But, no one flees very far. For a moment later curiosity again takes over. The warriors stand motionless watching the machine. The hum comes from the doorframe like part of the machine. There seems to be a green glow coming from the frame. Somehow there seems to be a picture forming in the frame. There is sheer amazement as the picture forms, the picture of a rolling green desert. The entrancing hum is broken by a "wheem" sound. Sword has hobbled into the building.

Sword: What's going on?

Arrow: Quiet.

Arrow moves toward the frame. He puts his hand through the frame.

Arrow: It's like a door.

Arrow cautiously steps through the door. He motions for the other warriors to follow.

Arrow: No Sword. Don't come through. You need to rest. There appears to be no danger here. It's just some kind of doorway.

Step: Arrow!

Step has stepped high into the air. And is calling from his vantage point.

Arrow: Yes.

Step: I see a group of people.

Arrow: What are they doing?

Step: They seem to be hiding and watching us.

The green light of the door reflecting off of the green desert sand was an eerie sight. The thought of others hiding and watching added to the eeriness of the situation.

Arrow: Let's go back. This thing must be guarded so that the hiding ones aren't tempted to come through.

That's when the situation became really spooky. The door disappeared. The green glow was missing from the night. As everything became dark even Arrow felt a tinge of fear. Alone in the Green Realm! In the Yellow Realm, Sword stands not knowing what to do...

The Next Morning in the Blue Realm

Hideo walks to school...

Hideo looks at the school and feels that he hasn't been here in a long time. It seems so familiar though. Just like the voice that greets him.

Hiroyuki: Hideo! Where have you been?

Hideo: Hi, Hiroyuki.

Hiroyuki: Hideo, why haven't you been coming to school?

Hideo doesn't answer.

Hiroyuki: Did your parents get on you? The principal called your house yesterday! And boy was she mad!

Hideo: Are you sure? I didn't know they called.

Hiroyuki: Your parents didn't say anything to you?

Hideo: No. Who is she?

Hideo's eyes catch the most beautiful girl that he's ever seen. Her hair is long and jet black.

Hiroyuki: What? She's a new girl. Her name is Samantha.

Hideo: She doesn't look Japanese.

Hiroyuki: She isn't. She's a foreigner. Hey, we better get to class.

Hideo: Oh yeah!

They break into a light sprint passing Samantha. Samantha looks at Hideo and smiles.

Hideo: Hiroyuki, she smiled at me.

Hiroyuki: Let's hope the teacher smiles at you!

Somehow Hideo doesn't care anymore.

The Yellow Realm, Maubuus' Castle...

Maubuus sits on his throne in obvious pain talking to himself.

Maubuus: Curse you warriors! Curse you all. You've taken the Machine of doors. How can I bring back my soldiers that you sent to the Red Realm? You will pay. You will pay! YOU WILL PAY!!

Maubuus insane scream echoes through the castle. Then he falls from his throne wracked by pain from the sword of Shatter.

The Green Realm

The three warriors are camped near where they came to this place. Each one took turns standing guard while the others slept. Now it is morning and they sit wondering what they'll do next.

Arrow: Step, check if we're still being watched.

Step once again attains his vantage point.

Step: I'd have to say, yes.

He motions towards the two individuals approaching. The three warriors watch silently. Wondering what will happen next. The two figures walk up to the warriors and immediately fall on their knees.

Barrier: What are they doing?

Step: Maybe they're tired of watching.

Arrow: Who are you?

Criz: We are of the tribe of Jethrel. My name is Criz. And this is wife Solana.

Arrow: I am Arrow. And this is Barrier and Step.

Barrier: Why have you been watching us?

Solana: You shine like the sun.

Criz: Nothing shines here except the sun. Be careful the Brigands will think you are friends of the one they hung.

Arrow: Someone shone like us. What is his name?

Criz: His name was Mist.

Arrow: These Brigands killed Mist?!

Criz: Not yet. They hung him on a cross as a symbol that no one should cross them. They keep him alive but he is near death now.

Arrow: These Brigands will pay if Mist dies!

Barrier: Why did they hang Mist?

Criz: He spoke out against the hunt.

Arrow ignores the "why." He is only concerned about Mist.

Arrow: Take us to Mist.

Criz: OK, but don't try to take him or the Brigands will attack you too.

Arrow: Take us to Mist!

The group begins to walk across the desert. Sometime later…

Criz: We found him bruised and battered after he came out of a glowing green doorway. His doorway was circular though. He was feeling better the next day. That day just happened to be the day of the hunt. Mist spoke against the hunt and angered the Brigand Masters.

Barrier: What do you hunt… people?

Criz: Yes.

Solana: There in the distance. There is Mist!

In a very barren place in the desert Mist could be seen hanging. There were two guards drinking water and joking near the cross.

Mist was hanging on what appeared to be a cross made out of dried cacti. The cacti here were large and seemed to have a rather woody nature to them.

Arrow fires a red arrow and hits one of the guards. The guard catches on fire. The other doesn't help. He sees the five figures coming and takes off running.

There seems to be fire in Arrow's eyes as he runs to Mist. Step and Barrier follow. Criz and Solana are hesitant. The burning guard is still screaming by the time Arrow arrives. Arrow completely ignores him as he takes Mist off the cross. He holds Mist body.

Mist: Oh...

Arrow: Where are the ones who did this to you?!

Step: I think they're coming.

Barrier: Where did they all come from?

Twenty men come running toward them. Solana and Criz drop to their knees.

Lead Brigand: Do you dare stand against the Brigands?

Arrow doesn't answer. He just lays Mist down.

Mist: I don't want to be left here. I want my blood to be buried with the ancestors.

Lead Brigand: Did you hear me?

All twenty men carry pole arms and crossbows.

Lead Brigand: I don't like the way you look! I don't like...

The lead Brigand doesn't finish his sentence as a yellow arrow rips through the Lead Brigand. The brigands charge Arrow. Step creates a step above Arrow's head. Arrow jumps up and pulls himself up just as the three brigands arrive. They crash into each other. Barrier charges into the crowd with a large barrier surrounding him. It knocks the brigands left and right as they hit against the barrier.

The brigands that are able scatter. They run in a helter skelter manner.

Mist: Arrow... Arrow.

Arrow: Yes, Mist. We are here.

Mist: I have to warn you...

Blue Realm...

It was the last class of the day for Hideo. The class was Psychology. It usually wasn't particularly interesting for Hideo but today the topic involved empathy.

Teacher: How many of you have seen those TV commercials where there are starving children in the 3rd world nations?

Almost the whole class raises their hand.

Teacher: Did you feel yourself in that situation?

Many students answer, "yes" in a mumbling wave that moves across the class. Then one student mentions that that's compassion not empathy.

Teacher: In part. How many of you have watched a movie and began to cry because of something that has happened in the movie? Or laugh because of something in the movie?

Student: Of course, we all have. It's just our attention being focused on a situation to the point where we believe it's true.

Teacher: To the point where you feel that you are that person.

Hideo: So, humans are empathetic creatures!

Hideo's outburst takes the class by surprise. The class laughs and the teacher smiles.

Teacher: Yes.

The bell rings at that moment. Immediately there is a shuffle of books and papers. And students head out the doors.

Hiroyuki: That was kind of strange how you suddenly just said that. What's going on?

Hideo: I just can't say.

Hiroyuki looks a little hurt but then he recovers.

Hiroyuki: Are you going straight home tomorrow?

Hideo: I was.

Hiroyuki: Let's go to the arcade. Samantha will be there and you can meet her.

Hideo: Why do you think that I want to meet her?

Hiroyuki just smiles.

Hideo: How did you know that she is going to the arcade tomorrow?

Hiroyuki: Her and my girlfriend seem to like each other. You're a lucky guy Hideo. So, I'll see you tomorrow. Oh, and try not to be too childish. She is a couple of years older than you!

Inside Hideo felt really excited. Things didn't seem so bad. So, Hideo headed home and his imagination took him over. He imagined what meeting the beautiful girl would be like. Imagining how he would say hello and how she would blush. And how gently they would fall in love.

...Elsewhere

Mist: This place will weaken you. Don't you feel weaker?

Arrow: ...I am hungry. We have not eaten.

Mist: No matter how much you eat your powers will grow weaker and a sense of exhaustion will... surround you.

Step: The bright sun and the green sand have affected his mind.

Mist: This is not a joke. In this world, there seem to be two classes of desert dwellers. One class a cruel hunter type group called the Brigands. The other group is the hunted group. They're like some kind light vampires. Just being around them will weaken you.

With these words, the warriors look around to see that Criz and Solana are gone. The three standing warriors look at each other in disbelief.

Arrow: Mist do you know where we can get some food and water.

Mist does not answer. He is dead.

Arrow: When the Doorway leaves...

Barrier and Step: All the warriors will die.

Yellow Realm

Sword: My sister is dead. My fellow warriors are far away somewhere! And I am stuck here.

Priest: The Gods and the ancestors have set your fate here. This is the place you must be. Heal yourself. Strengthen yourself. Be ready. You are a warrior. You will be called.

Sword: I will be ready! I will be ready!

The Blue Realm

The night was hard for Hideo. He had tossed and turned all night. It was torture. But he would never have traded it for anything. The day at school seemed to go so slowly too. As usual he didn't really pay attention because of his daydreams. Things were a bit different this time though. He wasn't daydreaming about heroic deeds and fantastic worlds. He was daydreaming about a woman that he was so strangely drawn to. That's why he found himself in the arcade now. Waiting for Hiroyuki, Hiroyuki's girl friend and Samantha.

Hideo: Maybe I should play a video game to calm down. When she comes I'll show her how good I am at some of them. She'll be amazed. She must like video games she wanted to come here.

Hideo surveys the rather large arcade. He wonders what he'll do first. Then he sees the Lord of the Dragon's pinball machine. In his dreams he always feared the dragon but the pinball machine made him feel superior to it. He walked toward the pinball machine with a familiar anticipation. He puts the money in and the machine comes alive.

Hiroyuki: Hey Hideo.

Hideo: Oh, hi Hiroyuki.

Hiroyuki is leading in two girls. One's his girlfriend Miki and the other is Samantha.

Hiroyuki: This is Samantha and Samantha this is Hideo.

Samantha: Hi.

Hideo: Hi.

Her eyes smile the word "hi" to him and his heart beats faster than ever before. As he looks at her the pinball goes into the hole.

Pinball Dragon: Ha ha ha!

Hideo gets snapped back to reality by the pinball machine's mechanical laugh.

Hideo: Ahh!

Everybody laughs. And Hideo blushes. Things weren't starting as he had imagined...

The Green Realm

Three lone souls trek across the green desert. All three are hungry, tired and thirsty.

Step: Arrow, the water is just up ahead.

Barrier: This is too spooky. Mist spoke of this place like it was highly populated but we haven't come to any settlements yet.

Arrow: Let's just keep going to the water.

Barrier: We're still going to need something to eat. I'm starving.

Coming over the last sand dune the water is in sight. The water is a welcome sight but no one has the strength to run to it. Step who is still in the air notices that another group is headed their way.

Step: We could have trouble. The group that was following us is definitely coming now.

Arrow: Let's get to the water before they do.

Arrow and Barrier do their best at running to the water while Step angles his steps toward the water. The warriors reach the water.

Arrow: Let me test the water.

Arrow takes a taste of the water and then smiles.

Arrow: It's alright.

The warriors begin to greedily gulp the little pond of water.

Barrier: The ones who followed us all last night will be upon us soon.

Arrow: Continue to drink. I will handle them.

Arrow looks into the distance behind the warriors. There he sees a band of about 10 - 20 people approaching. He can make out that Criz and Solana are among them.

Arrow watches until they are about 200 yards away.

Arrow: Stay away from us!

Arrow yells the warning. It almost seems like they don't hear him because they keep coming. Arrow waits. Barrier and Step lay exhausted beside the pond.

Arrow watches the group get closer. When they are about 150 yards away, Arrow begins to shine.

Arrow: I'm warning you!

Arrow fires an arrow of pure red light. It rips through the air. It flies near the group but doesn't hit any of them.

Arrow: You have been warned!

The group stops and sits on the sand.

Barrier: What are they doing?

Step: Maybe their feet hurt from all this walking. I know mine do.

Arrow: They are waiting.

Step: Look in the air. Birds!

Arrow looks up and fires an arrow without seeming to take aim. His arrow is on the mark. It brings down a bird. It crashes into the water. He fires again but the arrow doesn't make it to the birds. It fades before reaching them. Barrier and Step do not notice as they go to retrieve the bird. Arrow does notice though. Inside he knows that his power is getting weaker –just as Mist had said.

The Blue Realm

The day had been wonderful for Hideo. He had spent the whole day with his friends and Samantha. They had played video games, went out to eat together and had seen a movie. It was getting late but tomorrow was Saturday anyway.

Hiroyuki: I have to get home. I also have to take Miki home. Would you take Samantha home?

It was an obvious ploy to get the two together. Hideo was a bit shy but with Samantha things seemed to be so easygoing. She seemed endlessly interested in him. He told her things that other girls would have thought were stupid or weird. But she didn't. In only one night of fun he had told her some of the private thoughts that all people naturally guard especially an awkward teenager. He didn't know why. But he felt so comfortable with her.

Hiroyuki and Miki began to walk away.

Hideo: See you at school on Monday.

Hiroyuki: Does that mean that you are going to show up on Monday?

Hideo: Ha ha!

Hiroyuki: Have a good weekend!

Miki: Bye.

Hideo: Bye.

Samantha: Goodbye.

Hideo and Samantha stand watching Hiroyuki and Miki disappear into the distance of the night.

Hideo: I've never met a girl like you. You don't think that all my daydreaming is weird.

Samantha: A strong imagination is good. Those with good imaginations can always look at things in a new way.

Hideo: Look at things in new way. You don't know... you just don't know.

Samantha: You dream of being a great warrior but you only dream of being a warrior for good.

Hideo: Of course.

Samantha: How do you know what is good?

Hideo: I don't know. You just have to do what your heart tells you is right.

Samantha: What you think is right could cause a lot of harm though.

Hideo: But we are just talking about imagination.

Samantha: But imagination can just be practice for real life. You often have to imagine what you will do before you do it.

Hideo: Oh, you mean like you have to imagine how to handle a problem before you decide on the best course of action.

Samantha: Yes! Exactly!

Hideo: My daydreams involve strictly black and white issues. I fight evil. These are just daydreams! They aren't so important. I'm just trying to have an adventure.

Samantha: What you imagine tells me what kind of person you are.

Hideo: Do you really care?

Samantha: Yes. I do, Hideo.

She looks deeply into his eyes. And he looks deeply into hers. They're beautiful and concerned.

Hideo: Why are you suddenly so worried and so serious?

Samantha: I...I like you Hideo.

Those words send tingles through Hideo. -Tingles outstripping the slight chill on the wind.

Hideo: I like you too, Samantha. Can I see you tomorrow?

Samantha: I'm afraid not.

Hideo: Why?

She turns and runs. Hideo stands mystified for a moment. Then he chases her. She runs and turns a corner. Hideo turns the corner but when he does he doesn't see her. He just feels the chill of the night wind.

Hideo: Samantha! Samantha!

The Green Realm...

The mood had grown darker with the coming of the night. The warriors were vigilant of the 20 to 50 people sitting watching them. Their eyes seemed to be glowing a strange green color.

Barrier: That bird tasted good. I hope another flock flies overhead tomorrow.

Step: You were just hungry.

Barrier: Hungry and tired. I still don't feel rested with our friends just sitting out there. Arrow what are we going to do?

Arrow: For now, we're going to make our stand here! We have water and hopefully edible animals will come here looking for water.

Step: Hey Arrow. It looks like our buddies are on the move.

Green eyes attached to dark shapes could be seen to be rising. They cautiously trudged closer to the warriors.

Arrow: We are not kidding! Stay back!

Arrow rises and begins to shine. His shine isn't very bright though. Barrier and Step don't realize that he is struggling to maintain this glow. His characteristic bow and arrow appear.

Arrow: [Thinking to himself] My power is weakening. I have to kill as many as I can before my power is gone.

Arrow fires a red arrow at the closest of the vampire people. The arrow dissipates before it reaches him. He is about 90 yards away and the arrow only traveled about 80 yards. Barrier and Step notice that Arrow is weakening this time. They come to his side and begin to shine. They too feel how hard it is to even glow.

Barrier: They somehow sense how much power we have left. They stayed just outside your limit.

Step: Remember what Mist said about them draining your power by just being near you? Well maybe by them being near us they're somehow drinking our power.

Arrow: Well, it doesn't look like we're going to be able to run. Look...

Another group of the vampires have appeared on the opposite side of the pool of water. They too are about 90 yards away.

Step: This isn't too good guys!

Barrier: It may even be worse than you think. If they are somehow drinking our power then since there are two groups now we should weaken even faster!

Barrier: Arrow, what are we going to do?

Arrow doesn't answer. He just stares at the smaller group.

Barrier: What are we going to do?

Arrow: We're going to fight!

The two warriors stand dumbfounded.

Arrow: Gather as much water as you can.

The warriors gather water in the hollowed out cacti wrapped in pieces of their clothing. Arrow describes his plan as the two warriors gather water. By the time they're finished both groups of vampires have moved in 10 yards closer.

Arrow: This depends on you two guys.

All three warriors stand staring at the smaller group of vampires. After a while the vampires start to move forward again. The warriors charge the 20 vampires. The vampires look almost shocked. They stand watching. When the warriors reach the vampires. They let Barrier take the lead. Some of the vampires step forward to meet the warriors' insane charge. Suddenly Barrier shines as hard and as wide as he can. Five vampires slam into the Barrier. The barrier almost immediately disappears. Simultaneously a triple "wheem" sound is heard as 3 steps of light appear out of nowhere. The three warriors jump onto a light step. The steps have a springy nature to them. The warriors propel themselves over the vampires. Arrow fires two arrows in mid-air killing two of the vampires. The warriors crash into the sand a few yards away from the vampires. They right themselves and begin to run like the desert wind. The vampires begin to give chase. The warriors keep ahead of them though. The sound of squishy soft sand fills the night. It's like the sound of children running in snow -without the laughter. This is a land of horror.

The Blue Realm…

A week later, Hideo finds himself at the same place where Samantha disappeared. She hadn't come to school and no one knew where she had gone. She came into his life out of nowhere and she was gone just as quickly. He didn't really know her but everyday after school he found himself walking past this place. He felt so depressed. Home life wasn't good for him either. His grades were still suffering from all his daydreaming and his parents hated that. They let him know that by not mentioning it.

Hideo: I should have went to the Yellow Realm and checked on the warriors but I just didn't feel like it. I'll go this weekend. They probably don't need me since most of Maubuus' men are in the Red Realm. The warriors are OK. I don't want to go. If they need me they'll find some way to contact me.

Self-pity makes the final decision for Hideo.

The Green Realm…

One week had passed. One week of avoiding the Vampires and Brigands. One week of growing weaker and weaker. Their power had almost reached absolute zero. One use of their power was about all they could manage each day. They noticed that they were a lot more lethargic.

Barrier: We can't hold out much longer. We've just barely kept ahead of the vampires and Brigands. We have to find some way out of here.

Ahead of them lay a strange sight. It was a forest of cacti.

Arrow: It'll be cool there. Let's keep going.

The cacti were tall and provided shade. It didn't provide any respite from their aching muscles though. Suddenly,

Arrow: Warriors!

Barrier: What is it Arrow?

Arrow: We're being watched.

Step: I'm weak but maybe I could give you a bird's eye view.

Arrow: Don't waste your strength. I know they're here.

From above a Brigand jumps down knocking Barrier on the head. Barrier falls onto the hot sand. He lies there not moving. The Brigand pops up and yells out a strange war cry.

He makes the mistake of looking at Arrow. Arrow has made the sign of the hypnotic eye. The Brigand stares entranced. Until the fist of Step delivers him into the arms of sleep. Another Brigand jumps down onto Arrow. Arrow is slammed to the ground. Out of the fading light of evening, 5 more Brigands charge. A wild fistfight ensues. More Brigands come to join the fight. The warriors lose.

Lead Brigand: The two will be hung and this Arrow fellow will be part of our hunt!

Arrow is lying face down on the sand. The lead Brigand pulls his head up by the hair. Then he slams it back into the sand. The Brigands cheer uproariously!

The Blue Realm...

Hideo prepares for sleep. Another day has gone by. His mind is still fixated on Samantha.

Hideo: I've got to stop thinking about her. Everything about her was so strange though.

Hideo looks around the room for something to calm his weary mind. Beside his bed he sees a little notebook -the little notebook where he had written some of his wildest fantasies. He had thought that maybe it would make a good comic book someday.

He gets on his bed and flips through those familiar pages. His mind seems to be immediately engulfed in the comfortable excitement of the words. There he was a great hero. He always knew what to do in the pages. There he was saving the beautiful damsels! Of course there were parts with him battling great villains. Of course there was a part where he was a great leader on a campaign to slay an indescribably powerful dragon —whose claws could rip reality! Of course there were deeds greater than any man could do. When Hideo dreamed, he dreamed big!

These familiar daydreams lull him into the dreams of night where he finds himself standing beside the Old Doorway.

Hideo: You look sad.

Old Doorway: I'm tired.

Hideo: What have you been doing?

Old Doorway doesn't answer Hideo's question.

Old Doorway: My legs are tired.

Hideo: Have you been walking?

Old Doorway seems confused by the question.

Old Doorway: My legs are tired. Are your legs tired?

Hideo looks down at his legs. He notices that they are tired. He looks back up to tell Old Doorway but Old Doorway isn't there. To his side is Arrow. Arrow and Hideo are running.

Hideo: Why are we running?

Arrow doesn't answer. Behind him he hears the sound of beasts following him. He feels the sweat dripping from their tongues. He knows that he must run too. Arrow is fast but exhausted. Hideo glimpses at Arrow. And for the first time he sees fear in Arrow's eyes. Arrow turns and prepares to face the ones chasing him. The sheer exhaustion on his face is unbelievable. His sweat glistens in the cold moonlight.

The ones chasing come over the sand dune. Saliva is dripping from their mouths. The looks on their faces are insane. It's like the hunt has excited them into an animalistic frenzy. The crossbows and pole arms they carry seem to be the only hint of intelligence. They charge screaming. Strangely, Arrow doesn't move. And even stranger he doesn't shine. Many raise their crossbows and fire! The arrows zip toward him.

He's unable to react, move or shine. He just cries out with such emotion that Hideo cries out too.

Arrow: NO!

Hideo: NO!

WHEEM!!

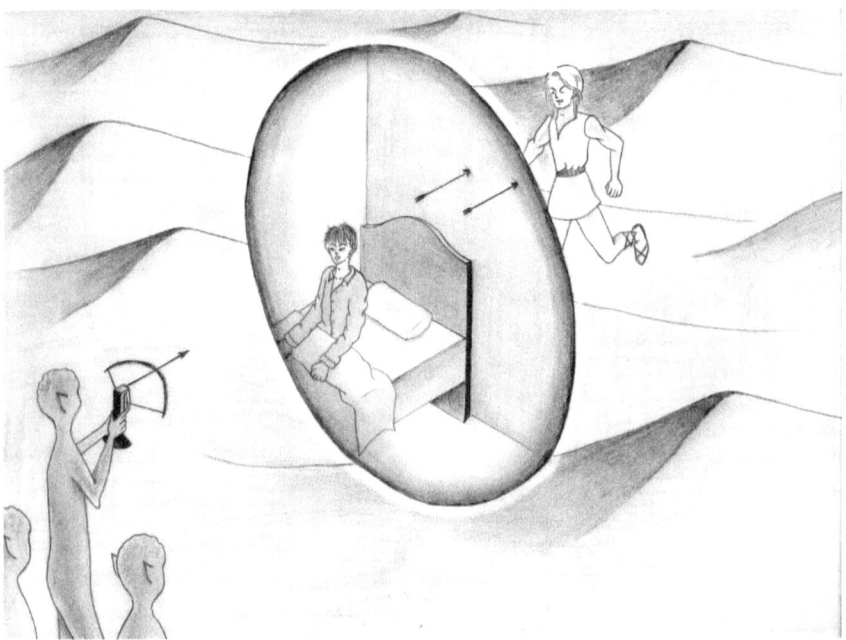

Their voices mix as a blue door flashes into reality. Hideo is ripped from sleep. The door appears in front of Arrow in the Green Realm. The arrows fly through it and exit in the Blue Realm as does Arrow but from the other side. The arrows lodge themselves into the wall above Hideo's bed with a series of heavy thuds.

Hideo ducks but sees Arrow come out of the other side of Green Realm door. The hunters are unsure what has just happened and stand dumbfounded for a moment.

Arrow: Close the door!

Footsteps shuffle toward Hideo's room. Hideo knows that they belong to his parents.

Hideo closes the door as the hideous faces run towards it.

Arrow: Yellow door now!

Hideo doesn't think. He just does what Arrow says. Somehow he knows exactly where to open the door and somehow he opens it perfectly. Arrow runs through the door grabbing Hideo and pulling him through too. The door collapses into a yellow light as Hideo's parents run into the room.

Mother: My God!

Yellow Realm...

Arrow: SWORD!

Sword comes running.

Arrow: Hideo, green door!

Again Hideo opens a green door. Arrow is glowing again. He seems almost vibrant.

The door opens in the camp of the Brigands. Barrier and Step are tied up. They look delirious.

Arrow fires angrily killing the Brigands. Sword does the same. The fighting ability is amazing -as is their cruelty. Hideo stands horrified. Then he runs and sets Barrier and Step free. Barrier and Step groggily step through the yellow door.

The cries of ferocity seem like distant echoes as Hideo steps into the yellow realm. Soon Arrow and Sword come through the door. Arrow is bloodied and his hair is a mess. But there is such a look of satisfaction on his face.

Hideo closes the door. He wanted his friends saved but he couldn't help but wonder if the events of tonight were right. So much has happened in such a short period of time. Hideo just feels drained.

CHAPTER 5

THE OLD WARRIORS

The warriors seem to get their strength back quickly.

Sword: What happened to you guys there?

Arrow: I don't know? All my strength was gone. I felt like an.

Hideo: An animal!

Arrow: I don't know what happened. I had to protect the warriors though. I had to protect... Hideo, you must remain with us.

Hideo: I'm sorry but I have a life on earth.

Arrow: This argument again! You are a Doorway! There must be a Doorway!

Hideo: Look; your legend says that "when the Doorway leaves all the warriors will die." Well, I left! You are still alive.

Arrow: We almost died!

Hideo: Almost. That means that the prophecy was wrong. Forget the old superstitions. Your whole world is not advancing. You're completely stuck with no innovation.

Arrow: What? We will follow the old ways!

Hideo: I looked around this village city the last time I was here. There is no advancement! Your people could be so much happier and so much safer if you would look to finding better ways of doing things. From my talks with Barrier I think your culture is older than the cultures of earth!

Sword: Earth?

Barrier: His home.

Arrow grimaces.

Arrow: The old ways work. They are all that is needed.

With that, Arrow storms off. Hideo feels anger with the way he was just dismissed by Arrow.

Hideo: I'm starting to hate him!

Barrier: He's just trying to say that he needs you.

Hideo: But what about my idea to advance your technology?

Barrier: Some have believed in trying new ways but they've always been proven foolish.

Hideo: On my world this place looks like something out of very early medieval times!

Barrier looks confused.

Hideo: And with what do you replace innovation? Superstition and backward tradition.

Barrier looks confused.

Hideo: You don't understand.

Barrier: Maybe you do not understand.

Hideo: What do you mean?

Barrier: Come with me.

Barrier was obviously tired. But he leads Hideo. They walk for about a half an hour.

Hideo: I'm tired and sleepy.

Barrier: I think I'm more so than you.

Hideo: Where are we going?! Can't I just open a door to wherever we're going?

Barrier: I am going to explain to you why Arrow is the way he is. Why we are the way we are. Now just follow me.

Barrier motions for Hideo to look straight ahead. Hideo looks. He only sees flat land with what seems to be some kind of markers. Then he realizes that...

Hideo: It's a graveyard.

There is a solemness in Barrier's eyes as he pulls out a bloodied piece of cloth.

Barrier: In the Green desert we found another warrior, Mist. I've brought his life here.

Hideo: His life? You mean his blood?

Barrier: His blood is his life. We bring the blood of our fallen warriors here for burial.

Hideo: You don't bury the body?

Barrier: Not here. Here is for the blood of the warrior.

Hideo: So his body is still in the Green Realm?

Barrier: Yes.

Hideo: But most of his blood is there.

Hideo turns and stares out over the flat plain. He stares at the many markers placed here.

Barrier: The life is in the blood. No matter how much or how little blood. The life is there. Honor is done to him by bringing his blood here.

Hideo: You bury it?

Barrier: I don't. I ---------.

The words of Barrier are unintelligible. So, Hideo turns but Barrier isn't there. Out of nowhere there is an old man to his far right.

Caretaker: Hi, I'm the caretaker here.

Hideo: Hi, you startled me.

The old man just stares at Hideo. He is slightly breathing out of his mouth.

Hideo: Did you see Barrier?

Caretaker: No, not yet.

Hideo looks puzzled.

Caretaker: Just a little joke.

Hideo: He came here to bring the blood of Mist.

Caretaker: Why else did he come?

Hideo: That's all.

Caretaker: No it isn't.

Hideo: What are you talking about?

Caretaker: Follow me.

Hideo takes another uneasy look around for Barrier.

Caretaker: Follow me. I have something to show you.

Hideo doesn't know what to do. So, he follows. Silently, they walk across the field of dead warriors.

Hideo: Where are we going?

Caretaker: Here.

His bony old finger points to a gravestone. Hideo leans forward to read the stone. Somehow, he slips on the dewy yellow grass. The grass is cool to his face and soft to the touch. Then he feels a very strong arm helping him to his feet. A very muscular powerful man stands there.

Hideo: Bolt?

Bolt: Of course Doorway.

Hideo: It's daylight!

Bolt: Afternoon to be exact.

Hideo looks around and sees that he's back in the city of the warriors. Bolt sees how confused he looks.

Bolt: Are you ok Doorway?

Hideo: Yes, my memory seems a little confused.

Bolt: We're really going to be needing you today. Maubuus has a powerful army in Sinder Forest. We can count on you, can't we?

Hideo looks at Bolt and sees that about 20 warriors are awaiting his reply.

Hideo: Of course! Have I ever let you down before?

Bolt smiles. He then turns and motions for all the warriors to gather. They all do. Hideo remains beside Bolt. Bolt begins to make a speech.

Bolt: We all know of the demon lights from the forest of Sinder. Well, it looks like Maubuus may be behind all of this. Our scouts say that Maubuus has men in this region. We are going to investigate. It's going to be dangerous. I've decided to take 6 warriors and Doorway with me. The six that I've chosen step forward.

From the crowd 6 warriors step forward and stand beside Bolt.

Bolt: The rest of you will protect the people until we return. Doorway...

As he says Hideo's name Hideo instinctively waves his arm. A yellow door opens. For the first time Hideo notices that his arm was different. In fact his whole body was different. It was like he was in another man's body. Living another person's life. Or maybe the thoughts of him being from the Blue Realm were all a dream. Through the door was a strangely dark forest.

Bolt: Keep your eyes out for Maubuus' men. They should be near here.

That's when the strange sounds boomed through the forest. They were the sounds of war. Bolt guided the warriors through the forest while watching out for Maubuus.

As they cautiously moved along, Bolt noticed movement in the forest to their left. Bolt made a motion and then everyone dropped down.

Hideo could see that it was another group of people. They seemed to be moving towards where the sounds of battle were taking place.

As he watched, he recognized one of the fighters. It was Maubuus! Maubuus had about 45 of his soldiers with him. Hideo could feel his heart start beating faster as Maubuus suddenly stopped.

Maubuus: Halt!

Maubuus looks around sniffing the air. And then he begins to laugh. The soldiers look puzzled.

Maubuus: I know that you're here. I can smell you! I can hear you breathing. Come out and face Maubuus.

There was an air of superiority in the way Maubuus always spoke. There was also a lusty thirst to kill that could be heard in his deep voice.

Bolt motioned for us to stay hidden. Then he arose.

Maubuus: Very heroic Bolt. I guess you will die today. Unfortunately, I don't have time to do it myself. Kill him.

Maubuus motions and 25 of his soldiers move toward Bolt with their swords drawn. Maubuus and the other 20 soldiers head off towards the incredible sounds and lights.

Bolt begins to shine. The usual "wheem" sound is drowned out by the ferocious sounds of battle.

Bolt stretches out his arm and a bolt of pure white energy comes out. It strikes 1 of the soldiers dead. The soldiers scatter so that they can attack from all sides. Bolt smiles and motions with his other arm for all the warriors to rise. The soldiers watch as this is done with the new shines preceding the warriors.

As the warriors shine, Hideo feels a closeness to them. He feels almost like he is each of them. He feels them as they instinctively form a circle around him. He is awash in the movement of their limbs as they slide into place around him. -The feeling of true empathy.

The soldiers viciously attack from all directions. Hideo is safe in the center. But all he can think about is the safety of the warriors. He opens and closes multiple doors all around the circle without thought. He can feel the needs of the warriors. A sword thrust that could not be avoided would be met by open door –seemingly out of nowhere. The whole group moved as one body. Their motion was liquid in nature. This was true empathy. For Hideo it was movement at the speed of thought. He was engaged and detached like flowing through a dream.

The warriors were outnumbered 3 to 1 but the circle remained unbroken! When the battle was over, not a warrior had fallen. Hideo had been in complete control of his power! He was amazed at his skill. He was so exhausted and exhilarated at the same time.

Bolt: Good job warriors! Now, let's see where Maubuus was headed.

So the group continues their little trek through the forest. After a few minutes they come to a clearing. The clearing was obviously unnatural. There were blast marks and burned plants all around. There were burned bodies too. Looks of sheer horror were on the faces of the dead men. Hideo could see the questions forming on all the warrior's faces.

Swish: What could cause something like this?

Bolt: I don't know. Maybe there were people with our shine. Maybe many gathered and fought here.

Into the clearing, steps Maubuus.

Maubuus: Well, I see that you've done away with the playmates I left you.

His men come out behind him. Many of them are carrying pieces of what looks like a machine of some sort.

Maubuus: Bolt! Do you dare face me?

Bolt: As all my ancestors, for all my ancestors, I stand against you!

Maubuus laughs and motions for his sword and shield. Maubuus' shield and sword are huge. Just looking at them you could tell they are at least

200 pounds each. Maubuus wields them as though they were as light as aluminum.

Maubuus' muscles were large and his skin had a scaliness about it. Almost like a reptile. Definitely his blood was colder than any reptiles had ever been. Bolt and Maubuus left their respective groups and met in the center of the charred black clearing.

It is then that Hideo catches sight of a strangely dressed man standing with Maubuus' group. He watches the events with a morbid fascination.

Maubuus and Bolt circle each other looking for a weakness or for fear. Neither have any. Maubuus swings his huge sword but Bolt is quick and easily moves. Bolt fires his bolt of energy but Maubuus blocks it with his shield. Bolt continues to fire but the shield was so thick Bolt couldn't penetrate it. This goes on for about 10 minutes. Then Bolt decides to fire at the ground under Maubuus. Bolt's energy cracks the ground and Maubuus falls! As Maubuus falls he throws his shield at Bolt. Bolt moves but his arm gets hit.

Bolt: Ahh!

Maubuus charges Bolt. They roll fighting on the ground. Maubuus is larger than Bolt and begins to gain the upper hand. He is knocking Bolt around. Then he moves in for the kill. But Bolt isn't finished. He begins to shine again. He lets go with a bolt of energy that blasts Maubuus. Maubuus is obviously hurt. And Bolt obviously has no more strength to fire energy. Both stagger dazed. Bolt staggers toward the sword that Maubuus dropped.

The strangely dressed one sees this and yells to Maubuus. He throws Maubuus a small object. Maubuus catches it and turns to Bolt. Then there is a flash of light from Maubuus and Bolt burst into flames. The warriors look on in horror unable to do anything. Fear fills everyone. And Bolt falls dead!

Maubuus stands up and just laughs at the flaming body.

Suddenly Maubuus stops laughing and stares an insane stare at the warriors. A flash of light flashes out again. Hideo thoughtlessly opens a door and saves the life of Swish.

Hideo: Through the door warriors!

Hideo opens a door so that all the warriors can go through. The surviving warriors rush through the door. Hideo is the last to go through the door. Hideo stops and looks at Maubuus. He just freezes and looks at the evil eyes of Maubuus. Maubuus seems to be moving in slow motion. Maubuus slowly raises the object and points it at Hideo. Hideo doesn't move. There is almost a conversation in the connection of their eyes.

Then Maubuus turns the weapon away and points it at the strangely dressed guy. The strange one has fear in his eyes one moment and then he is dead the next. Hideo stands there puzzled. Maubuus turns back to Hideo and smiles.

Hideo turns and slowly walks through the door. He feels confused but he knows what Maubuus pointed at him. It was a gun. Hideo knew that but he didn't say anything. He just quietly listened as the warriors explained to the people what had happened. He just quietly followed as the warriors went to the wife of Bolt and explained to her that her husband was dead.

There wasn't even blood to take to the graveyard. There was a special ceremony held the next day where Bolt's only child gave some of his blood in his father's stead. It was truly a sad scene. To see the little six-year-old get his palm ritualistically cut. The little boy seemed to have almost no emotion as the ceremony took place. Even when they cut him, he kept a face a stone.

Bolt's Wife: No!! Why! Why! Bolt I love you! Ah! Ahhh! Ahh!

The little boy's face changes and he runs over to his mother. She gets up and runs across the field of graves. She runs towards Sinder Forest. No one stops her. No one dares! She was the wife of the greatest warrior there had ever been -a warrior that had fought many valiant battles.

No one stopped her. It almost seemed an act of respect. She ran off and Hideo felt her despair. More so did he feel the despair of the little boy who would see his mother for the last time that day.

Hideo: My God! My God!

Hideo falls to his knees crying. His palms cover his face but the tears stream through. A strong hand touches his shoulder trying to comfort him.

Barrier: Hideo? Hideo? Are you ok?

Hideo: Barrier? Huh?

Hideo looks around and sees that he and Barrier are the only ones there. Also, it isn't daytime. It's early morning.

Barrier: Hideo, why are you crying?

Hideo: Maubuus killed Bolt.

Barrier: What? Yes, about 20 years ago. How did you know that?

Hideo: I...I don't know. But I know I have to help you. I think I've been shown some very important things. I think I know what happened at the Battle of the Fire!!...Where were you?

Barrier: I walked away to find the caretaker so that a marker could be made for Mist. When I returned I saw you walking away mumbling to yourself. I called out but you didn't hear me. Then you fell at the grave of Bolt.

Hideo: I think I saw the past. I mean I saw what happened in your past!

Barrier looks at Hideo strangely.

Hideo: You have to believe me. Ah... was there a battle in Sinder Forest?

Barrier: Yes, there have been a few.

Hideo: I mean about 20 years ago.

Barrier: Yes.

Hideo: This is the battle where Bolt died.

Barrier: Yes but everyone knows that. He was one of our greatest warriors.

Hideo: Every one of your people knows that. But not me.

Barrier: Did someone tell you?

Hideo: No! I saw it!

Barrier is a man of superstition but still he is skeptical.

Barrier: You looked like you hit your head pretty hard when you fell. Are you sure someone didn't tell you...

Hideo: Listen, how well do you remember that battle?

Barrier: I was a warrior at the time but I didn't go with Bolt.

Hideo: Oh yeah! That's right. I didn't see you among those chosen. Anyway I saw...

Around noon that next day all the warriors are gathered and listening to Hideo.

Hideo: I saw Maubuus in Sinder Forest. He shot Bolt with some kind of gun.

Everyone looks confused.

Sword: What is a gun?

Hideo: It's mechanical device that hurls a projectile at a target.

Everyone looks very confused.

Hideo: Let me put it this way. It's like a special bow and arrow. This bow fires arrows of light that can hurt.

Arrow: Like my power.

Hideo: Yes, YES! Exactly! This bow is smaller though and made of metal or plastic.

Arrow: Plastic?

Hideo: OK...metal. It's made of metal. You can shoot it with one hand. Firing it is controlled by a finger.

The warriors look amazed.

Barrier: This is a weapon so it would never get tired.

Hideo: Yes! And the light it fires burns. You told me stories about how at the battle of the fire there was fire all around. It came from the sky. There was fire all around. You're not sure of what exactly happened. You don't have the words to explain what you saw.

The warriors stare in silence.

Hideo: Don't you see? Maubuus has technology…uh special weapons.

Sword: We've never heard of him using the power against us before.

Arrow: He never has. We know his tactics. We know how he fights wars. We know our history! The Fire was the first time something like this happened. If Maubuus has these special weapons then why doesn't he use them all the time?

Step: Maybe he has a kind side that we just don't see so much.

A small laugh ripples through the warriors.

Arrow: Hideo, answer my question.

Hideo: I..I don't know. I can't explain why he doesn't always use his weapons. Maybe he first got them at the Battle of Sinder Forest. His people were carrying pieces of metal.

Sword: That's still 20 years without using his weapons.

Arrow: Many things don't make sense.

Hideo: Many more things do make sense though. He has weapons that you don't know about!

Sword: So, he has things that we don't know about. What is the point of this?

Hideo: I want to help. I want to even things up. I can get you weapons here!

Arrow: We have our tried and true methods of fighting. We don't need any special weapons.

Hideo: You're prejudiced against weapons because they aren't traditional! And because I'm an outsider. If Maubuus has weapons and you don't then what will you do?

Arrow: The same thing we always have...fight and win.

Hideo: Old Doorway gave me his power. Maybe this is why I was shown what happened 20 years ago. My thinking is different. I understand technology. Maybe this is why the Power Transfer Ritual didn't work. My job here isn't finished yet!

Arrow: [laughing] Are you going to save us?

Hideo: Without me all the warriors die according to your own myth. This is important. Maybe it was your ancestors or God that showed me these things. I think I'm supposed to be here now! I want to help!!

Arrow: This is a very big change Hideo. Aren't you worried about school or your parents?

Hideo: Of course I am!

The passion in their voices can be felt -each side arguing his point.

Arrow: Then why the big change?!

Hideo: Because of what I saw! It wasn't the death and the violence that got me. It wasn't the selfless courage and comradery either. It...it was the eyes of a small child that lost his father to Maubuus and his mother to insanity. A little boy who stood there behind a shield of emotionlessness as he gave his blood in memory of his father, Bolt! I felt empathy like never before. I felt the fear and sadness in his heart! The ONLY son, now completely alone.

Barrier: You're crying now as you were in the cemetery.

Hideo: I can feel that moment again. I can feel that empathy again! I've got to help. I can't let the viciousness of Maubuus rule here!

Hideo looks pleadingly at Arrow. A look that was akin to the heart asking the brain to fulfill a grand wish. Arrow's face seems to sadden.

Arrow: I will consider your offer.

Arrow walks out the door.

Hideo: I just don't understand him!

The warriors disperse and begin heading out the door.

Hideo: Look at the dangerous situation here. Maubuus could have very advanced weapons! Arrow will never understand what I felt.

Step stops.

Step: I think he does understand. He has to. He is Bolt's son.

Walter Pierce

CHAPTER 6

AMERICA

The council is again meeting. This time they are listening to an expert on the warriors explain their powers.

Dr. Sems: The remaining warriors consist of Arrow, Barrier, Sword, Step and Doorway. They all have powers based on frequencies of light.

Councilman 1: They also have a hypnotic eye power.

Dr. Sems: Yes, I was just about to get to that. The hypnotic eye is a power that they all seem to share. It seems that once a warrior comes of age to manifest their powers, the hypnotic eye naturally comes also.

Councilman 1: Do any of the other peoples on this planet display this power?

Dr. Sems: No. We have not found another race that displays this ability. We haven't been able to genetically reproduce this ability either.

Councilman 2: Are there any of the warrior's people that display this hypnotic ability?

Dr. Sems: Well generally no. In the past there were unconfirmable reports that some of the people were displaying this ability without having a power of light.

Councilman 3: Can we get on with the description of their specific known powers!

Dr. Sems: Of course. Arrow has displayed 4 varieties of arrows, Yellow, Green, Blue, and Red. Yellow has a powerful slicing effect. It can cut through some very dense objects. Green has an electrical affect on most creatures. It kills through the destruction of the nervous system. Blue has a stunning effect on most creatures. Red has...

As the doctor continues explaining, he is interrupted by Jethri.

Jethri: Council! I must speak with you! The worst possible thing has happened.

Councilman 3: What is so important that you are brave enough to interrupt an official meeting of this council! Your explanation had better be good!

Jethri: It is. Hideo is the one that was predicted to come.

Dr. Sems: What?

Councilman 1: Please excuse us Dr. We will continue this briefing at a later time.

The Dr. looks confused and heads for the door.

Councilman 2: Oh doctor...don't mention anything that has happened here to anyone else. Do you understand me?

Dr. Sems: Yes.

The doctor exits.

Councilman 3: Now what are you babbling about?

Jethri: Hideo is going to bring technology to the warriors. He wants to introduce guns!

The council looks on in silent disbelief.

Jethri: Look at what that would do to the warriors. With the right weapons they could pose a threat to us!

Councilman 3: The time has come to act!

Maubuus' Castle…

Maubuus' last 2 wizards stand looking out the castle window.

Robius: Maubuus' condition gets worse and worse. We have no way to stop this infection.

Milstar: Yes…

The two wizards burst into uncontrollable laughter.

Robius: Maubuus will do unspeakable horrors to the last warriors if he ever gains enough strength to mount an attack.

Milstar: Our lives may actually be quiet for a while.

Robius: Our 5 brother wizards are dead, a good portion of Maubuus' army is trapped in the Red Realm, and Maubuus is injured. I think things are pretty bad for Maubuus' desire for conquest! Which all means that we get to rest for a while.

The door to the room bursts open. Standing there is Maubuus.

Maubuus: Do you think that I am weak!

Robius: No, lord Maubuus.

Milstar: No, my lord.

The fear can be heard in the wizards' voices.

Maubuus: Down on your knees!

The two wizards drop to their knees.

Maubuus: I am surrounded by weakness! Milstar!

Milstar: Yes, master.

Maubuus: Call the birds, Robius!

Robius: Yes, master.

Maubuus: Gather the assassins.

City of the Warriors...

Arrow enters the room again.

Arrow: I've decided that we will use the guns that Hideo will introduce.

Hideo: Great! Do you have money? Of course not. Do you have anything valuable like gold?

Arrow: We can get you gold. Some of the caves near Sinder Forest have gold. I, Hideo and a couple townspeople will go and get the gold. Barrier, Sword, and Step will remain here.

A little later near Sinder Forest...

Hideo: After we get the gold we'll go to a place in my realm named America. I have a cousin there.

Arrow continues to work as he listens, picking up gold nuggets off the cave floor.

Hideo: He'll help me exchange the gold for money. Then I just have to find a place where I can buy a gun. I've never been to America...

Arrow stops working.

Arrow: America? That name is familiar.

Hideo: What? Really? Where did you hear it?

Arrow: I'm not sure.

Hideo: It must just sound like one of your words.

Arrow doesn't answer.

Hideo: Arrow... may I ask you a question? What happened to your mother? I saw her run off.

Arrow: She never came back.

Hideo: Did you search for her?

Arrow: No.

Hideo: Why not?

Arrow: These guns will make my people powerful?

Arrow's change of subject is abrupt. Hideo is still curious but not willing to anger Arrow by asking again.

Hideo: Yes. All of your people can be warriors if they have guns.

Arrow: We can finally be safe from Maubuus?

Hideo: Yes.

Arrow: This is good.

They continue examining the rocks for traces of gold.

Arrow: Hideo do you care about my people?

Hideo: Yes. I can feel them now. It's like they're a part of me. I especially feel the warriors though.

Arrow: I was too young at first.

Hideo: What?

Arrow: The reason I didn't search for my mother... Then we all assumed she was dead.

Hideo: Do you blame her for leaving?

Arrow: I blame Maubuus! I will kill him! I couldn't protect my father and I couldn't protect my mother. But I will protect my people!

Hideo: Wow, calm down Arrow.

Arrow: Maubuus took everything from me! I won't let him harm the people! I'm not helpless anymore!

Hideo: How old is Maubuus?

Arrow: He has been around since the beginning.

Hideo: What do you mean?

Arrow: He is very old.

Hideo: How old? A hundred?

Arrow: Much older.

Hideo: Three hundred?

Arrow: Over a thousand but I don't know how much.

Hideo: How old do you people get here?!

Arrow: Maubuus is different from us. Just his looks tell you that he is... unnatural.

Hideo: This is a strange place.

Arrow: Do we have enough gold rocks now?

Hideo: Yeah, I think this should do.

Arrow motions for the two townspeople to take the small sacks of gold out of the cave.

Hideo: Next, we have to pick out the purest rocks. Then I'll go to America. This time when the Doorway leaves the warriors won't die. They'll grow in number!

Arrow doesn't like the joke.

Arrow: Don't make light of our old sayings... wait that's where I heard the term America. It was in a story my father told me, the story of the baby bird. When he was a child some of the warriors passed through the blue realm to escape Maubuus. One among the warriors was named Vision. When she shined she could put her mind wherever she pointed her light. It was like seeing and being there at the same time. When they went through the blue realm something reflected light in the sky. The warriors were already very agitated and Vision instinctively shone towards the thing in the sky to see what it was. She saw a silver bird. The bird gave birth in the air! When the bird gave birth a word flashed into Vision's mind. That word was America. The baby's name was America.

Hideo: What a strange story.

Arrow: It gets stranger. The bird gave a great cry and there appeared a tree in the sky to give the bird rest. And then the bird showed its power. It made it rain! And then the rain turned black!

Hideo: Do you really believe that? The bird had magical power? That's ridiculous. The first part of the story sounded like a plane but the rest is fantasy.

Arrow: What's a plane?

Hideo: Never mind. I suppose the originators of this story are long since dead. That's how myths and legends get started. A story gets changed over time.

Arrow ignores the final part of Hideo's words. He's a bit indignant that Hideo has discounted his story.

Arrow: Yes, they're dead now. They only lived about a week after the battle with Maubuus. Maubuus somehow scourged them. Their hair started falling out and burns developed on their bodies. It was horrible.

Hideo's eyes change from disbelief to concern.

Hideo: What did the tree look like?

Arrow stoops down and draws in the dirt. Hideo looks at the drawing with horror.

Hideo: I can't. I can't get guns for you.

Arrow looks up shocked by what he's just heard.

Arrow: Are you joking?!

Hideo: I can't lead you down this path.

Arrow: What about my people? You don't care what becomes of us! You would leave us vulnerable to Maubuus' attack! Just tell me why?

Hideo: I can't explain.

Tears begin to well up in Hideo's eyes. Arrow looks on angrily. From past encounters, Arrow knows that it is useless to try to influence Hideo. In despair and disgust Arrow turns and heads out the cave. Hideo turns and looks at the drawing on the ground. It is undeniably a mushroom cloud.

CHAPTER 7

THE SCIENTISTS

Hideo looks up from the ground. There he sees the shadow of Arrow just outside the cave entrance.

Hideo: I have to explain.

Out of nowhere, a flash of light engulfs Hideo. The flash startles Arrow who glimpses it out of the corner of his eye. He turns and looks into the cave. He sees that Hideo is not there.

Arrow: Hideo?

Hideo wakes up strapped to a laboratory bed. There are two men standing near him dressed like doctors.

Dr. Herzt: It appears to be waking up.

Dr. Carr: His anatomy is very similar to that of the warriors. The brain seems to be nothing special except that it's divided into two hemispheres.

Dr. Herzt: Now that it is awake we can begin mapping the centers of its brain.

Hideo: What? Who are you? Let me go!

Dr. Herzt: He doesn't seem so disoriented. Let's give him another shot.

Hideo struggles to free himself as one of the doctors approaches him with a needle. That is when Hideo begins to shine. He opens a door between him and the doctor. As the doctor moves to one side, Hideo moves the door to the same side.

Dr.Herzt: Stop this nonsense and let me give you the shot!

Hideo is so focused on Dr. Herzt that he doesn't notice that Dr. Carr has moved to his other side with another needle. Hideo only feels a moments worth of pain as he is injected. Then everything just seems dreamy and unfocused. He feels happy to just watch the pretty colors play in front of his eyes.

Dr. Herzt: We are really going to have problems with this one.

Dr. Carr: The fools on the Council don't realize what they've done. They have kidnapped a Doorway! The warriors would give their last ounce of blood to protect this one. Without him they believe their civilization will come to an end! From our studies, you can see that they are fiercely superstitious!

The two men turn to Hideo who is happily staring at the white walls.

The next days are not happy for Hideo. He is tested and prodded to excess. He would be in extreme pain if it were not for the fact that he is constantly under the affect of drugs. A stupor that keeps him only partially aware of all the things that are happening. He can't quite piece together these days. He wonders if he is crazy. The things he's seen, the things he's done, they all seem so unbelievable. The only way for him to keep sane is to try to keep the events of each day remembered. And then try to sort the real events from the drug in induced hallucinations. He knows that the days consist of scheduled tests, 3 feedings, and a time for exercise. All of these things seem to be real. There is also one other thing that seems to be real but he has no idea how it could be. He's sure he's met Samantha.

Council Meeting...

Jethri: The warriors have been scouring the areas near the cave for Hideo. They are even beginning to overcome their fear of the deeper recesses of Sinder forest! They could actually discover us! This course of action has made the situation worse.

Councilman 3: He should be killed now!

Councilman 1: Exactly the opposite should be done! He should be returned to the warriors.

Councilman 2: Dr. Carr will bring Hideo here soon.

At that moment Dr. Carr enters the room.

Councilman 2: Have you learned anything from Hideo?

Dr. Carr: He doesn't have any special abilities beyond those of a Doorway. His physical strength is far below that of a warrior. His reflexes aren't really that well developed and he has no formal training in combat. Why he was chosen, I do not know.

Jethri: I witnessed the power transfer. The warriors actually tried to take the power from him but were unsuccessful.

Councilman 1: What do you mean unsuccessful?

Jethri: They just weren't able to do it.

Councilman 2: Bring this Hideo in.

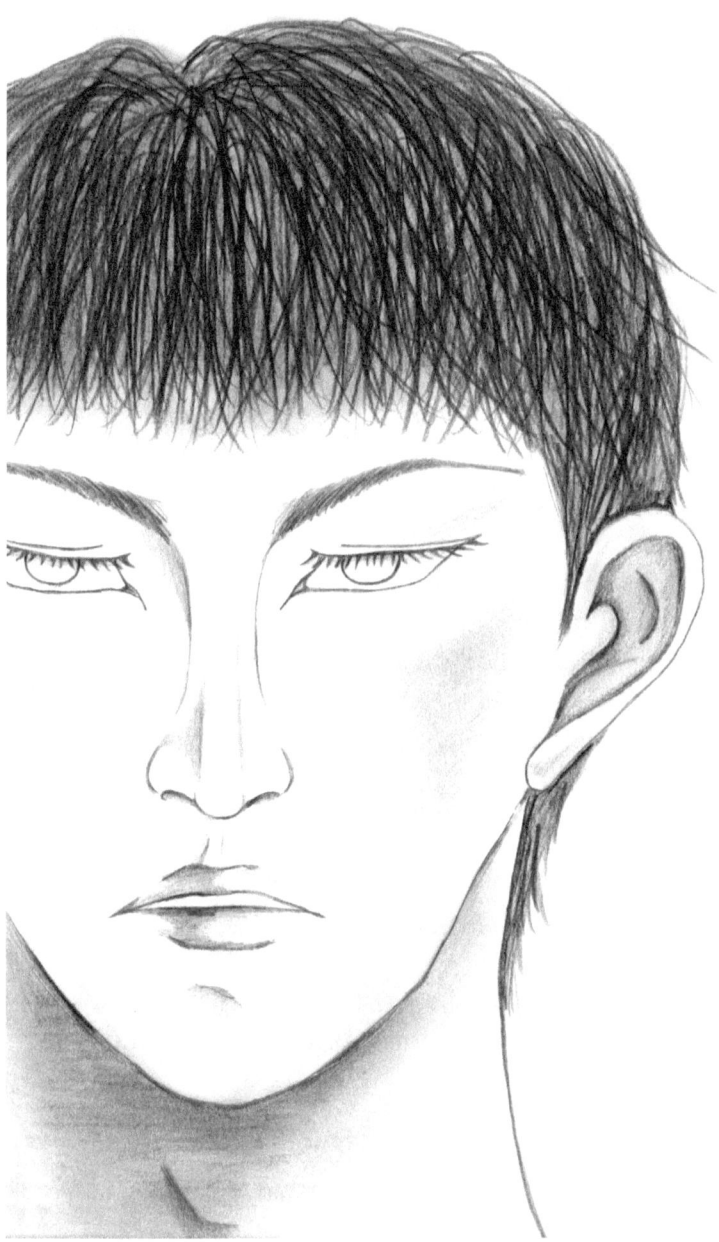

Dr. Carr exits and returns. He returns leading Hideo in. Hideo is obviously in a daze.

Hideo: Is this real? This is not part of the usual schedule.

Hideo staggers as he walks. He waves to the members of the council.

Councilman 2: Bring him out of the stupor.

Dr. Carr: I don't know if that is wise sir. He may be able to shine.

Councilman 2: Bring him out. But keep the drugs ready.

Hideo feels his ability to think return. He feels like he's a part of the world again.

Hideo: Where is this place?

Councilman 3: You are in a place where we ask the questions.

Hideo could understand. Even under the drugs he could sometimes understand words. But now he could understand words and the extra little meanings contained in how the words were spoken. He understood that he was to only answer their questions and he felt the arrogance that was clear in the tone of the words.

Councilman 2: Do you plan to bring technological weapons into this realm?

Hideo: I was planning to but I decided against it.

Jethri: What he is saying sounds correct. Just before I stunned him he told Arrow that he would not introduce guns into this realm.

Councilman 3: Wise choice!

Councilman 2: Hideo, we protect this planet. We ... guide it. We do not let outsiders interfere in its development.

Councilman 1: Why are you here Hideo?

Hideo: You brought me here.

Councilman 1: No, I mean this realm.

Hideo: I've asked myself that many times.

Councilman 3: Answer our questions!

Hideo: I... am helping the warriors.

Councilman 1: What do you think of us?

Hideo: I don't know anything about you.

Councilman 3: Why do you want to kill us?

Hideo: What? I don't want to kill you. I know nothing about you!

Councilman 3: Don't lie to me!

Hideo: I'm not lying!

Hideo can hear the seriousness and anger in the councilman's words. Hideo feels so confused. He watches helplessly as the councilmen begin conferring amongst themselves.

Councilman 1: How many weapons do you have access to?

Hideo: I'm not really sure. I guess that I'd be able to get as many as I could buy.

Councilman 2: How many did you plan to buy?

Hideo: I don't know. Ahhh!

Hideo has been talking with pain in his body from the medical tests. But now a sharp pain shoots through his arm.

Councilman 1: Why is it yelling?

Dr. Carr: Forgive me sir. It is a side effect of some of nerve tests that we conducted.

Hideo feels angry. They are talking about him as if he is an animal.

Hideo: What gives you the right to treat me like this?!

Dr. Carr: Quiet!

Hideo: No! You've tested me, drugged me and played with my body as if I were some lab rat!

The councilmen look worried and begin to confer again.

Councilman 1: How many soldiers could you bring into this realm from yours?

Hideo: You're afraid of me. You act so mighty and smug but you're afraid of me! I'm nothing but a high school student! I'm no general! I don't command armies!

Councilman 3: Bring in Sadastra.

The beautiful young Sadastra enters the room. Hideo can't believe his eyes. For he knew this woman as Samantha.

Hideo: Samantha?!

Sadastra: Yes, Hideo. But my real name is Sadastra.

Hideo: You're one of them?

Sadastra: Uh...

Councilman 2: Does he have any military connections?

Sadastra: No. As I've told you before, he was simply a student. He didn't even have many friends. I really don't think he is a threat.

Hideo: I'm really tired of Ahh... I'm not going to answer any more questions!

Councilman 3: You will!

Hideo: Why? What do I have to gain! I feel that I'm just an animal to you!! I won't help you!

Councilman 2: I'm sorry. We will explain.

Councilman 3: Councilman?!

Councilman 2: I think that he must understand our position. We are a people of science. Our people are not a warlike people. We have certain technologies that allow us to peer into the future. On a certain date in the not too distant future our people here will be destroyed!

Hideo: Who destroys them?

Councilman 2: That is what we don't know. It takes a great amount of energy for us to make a very short jump into the future. The closer the jump is to the present the less amount of energy we need. Unfortunately this is still a vast amount of energy and we won't be able to produce that amount until a day or two before the date.

Hideo: So, you think that I am the one who will destroy your civilization?

Councilman 1: You are the one variable here... the unknown element.

Councilman 3: No power here is strong enough to destroy us.

Councilman 2: The warriors don't know we exist and they would easily be overwhelmed by our technology and numbers.

Councilman 3: Maubuus is vicious but he too would be overwhelmed by our force.

Councilman 1: The sundry other little tribes that Maubuus hasn't taken over pose absolutely no threat.

Hideo: What about a combination of all the forces?

Councilman 3: Still no threat. But a large military invasion from the Blue Realm could overwhelm us. Before you came there was no chance of us being beaten but suddenly it is possible.

Hideo: But why would I?

Councilman 1: We don't know. After evaluating you we don't think that you are a threat. Maybe you are not the one who causes the destruction but you are just the most obvious choice.

Councilman 2: Now we have to decide whether to kill you or...

Hideo: What?

Sadastra: Please let him go. He's no threat.

Councilman 3: Shut her up.

Sadastra: I'm sorry but...

Dr. Carr slaps Sadastra.

Dr. Carr: Shut up!

Hideo: Leave her alone!

Hideo attacks Dr. Carr. He easily knocks Dr. Carr to the ground with one hit. Dr. Carr's holds his bloody nose while looking up at Hideo. Hideo holds Sadastra behind him.

Two armed guards rush into the room. Hideo tries to shine but isn't able to.

Councilman 1: Put Hideo back into his cell!

A flash of light from the guard's gun engulfs Hideo.

Hideo awakes in pain, in his cell again. Hours pass. Hideo somehow realizes that this is about the time he gets his next shot of drugs. He hears the doctor and a couple of guards enter the room. He is still far too drugged to do anything about it. He can't even see them. He can only hear them. The footsteps get closer and closer to him. Now he can smell their chemical clean smell.

Next he feels their cold hands grab him. Their sterile emotionlessness filters through his stupor. They hold out his arm. He expects to feel the pinching pain next but instead he hears a whistling sound. He feels a cold wind. The wind knocks him against the wall. He slides down the wall. He can see shadows moving and can hear thuds against the walls. Then there is a soft voice... the voice of Sadastra.

Sadastra: I have to get you out of here.

Sadastra injects him with another dose of drugs.

Sadastra: This will counteract the drugs they've used on you.

The next events are very hazy. He remembers running through corridors sneaking past guards and feeling strong winds. He could hear footsteps constantly approaching.

Finally, he felt his back against a wall with guards approaching. Little by little Hideo could feel power returning.

He strained but he knew that he could not open a door. He almost felt like crying as he realized that he was going to have more torture at the hands of these cold hearts.

Hideo: I won't go back!

There's a wheem but the door doesn't open. It's just a ball of light spinning. Then he feels the warm hand of Sadastra. A tingle runs through his body and the door opens!

Sadastra pulls him through and the door closes immediately.

In the World of Dreams…

Hideo falls through a chasm of darkness.

Hideo: Ahh!

He's given up hope. He feels that he will forever be locked inside himself with these drugs. He lands on an open plain and wildly runs across the land. A pack of wolves join him. He feels so free. No coherent thoughts. Nothing in his world is logical. He simply exists! The further he runs the deeper he goes into the arms of madness. And he just doesn't care!

The wolves stop at a lake to water themselves. He enjoys frolicking in the in the water. Then there is that silent call -the call for the wolves to again run. He runs with all his heart. The cool wind rips at his humanity. Sanity disappears in the embrace of darkness. He runs further and further feeling his shape changing to that of a wolf. But then he hears a voice…

Old Doorway: Hideo, I am here.

Hideo: Grrr…

Old Doorway: Hideo you must fight.

Hideo lunges at the old man. He wants to rip him to shreds. He hits the old man and knocks him to the ground.

Old Doorway motions with his hands.

Old Doorway: This is the hypnotic eye.

Hideo looks on intrigued.

Old Doorway: All of our people are immune to it.

Hideo watches and uses his intellect to understand the words.

Old Doorway: The champions of our people have the power of the hypnotic eye.

Hideo's body is that of a man again. He gets off of Old Doorway and helps him up.

Hideo: I'm sorry. I don't know what I was doing.

Old Doorway: You must wake up.

Hideo: How can I?

Old Doorway: You must try! I will help you.

Hideo tries and feels himself rising out of sleep. The struggle is tremendous. Trying with all his heart to push across that line of consciousness. That's when he is pushed across by the old but strong hands of Old Doorway.

CHAPTER 8

THE MADMAN

There are unseen eyes in a forest. Eyes that are always watching. These are the eyes of birds. They watch a young woman gently guiding a young man. The man's name is Hideo Nakamura and the woman is called Sadastra.

The birds watch the tortured steps of Hideo. They are ever mindful of possible danger. There is another pair of eyes watching. A pair of evil eyes that are thoroughly enjoying what they are seeing. The eyes belong to Milstar, a wizard of King Maubuus.

Milstar sits in meditation linked to the birds. He is focusing all his awareness through the eyes of one of the birds. His heart is overjoyed that he has found the target of his search. He is doubly pleased that his target is hurt and nearly alone. With a deep breath the link to the birds is broken.

Milstar: Now to tell King Maubuus the news.

He gets up and stretches. He makes his way through the castle to the royal chamber of Maubuus. 7 guards block the way but they quickly part for one of Maubuus' wizards. Resolutely Milstar continues on. He momentarily bows to one of Maubuus' many sons as he passes. Finally, he arrives at the bedside of Maubuus.

Half of Maubuus' flesh seems to be rotting. The simple shard of Shatter's Sword has spread to 40% of Maubuus' body.

Milstar: I've found Doorway.

Maubuus: Yes.

Milstar: He is with a woman in Sinder Forest. He is vulnerable.

Maubuus sits up. He has an insane look in his eyes.

Maubuus: Send the assassins!!

The Council...

The council is convened

Councilman 3: Did we do the right thing?

Councilman 2: Only time will tell.

Councilman 3: Letting Hideo go was bold.

Councilman 1: We got the information that we needed. He doesn't seem to be a threat at all but we'll monitor the situation closely. With more facts now, we can better make decisions.

Councilman 3: But what if Hideo tells the warriors about us?

Councilman 2: They won't understand. They'll just think there is a group with powerful magic living in Sinder Forest. They've believed this for a long time there is no conflict.

Councilman 1: Once Hideo returns to the warriors they will stop their frenzied searches through the forest. A semblance of normality may return to this place.

Sinder Forest...

The medicine that Hideo was given is finally wearing off. He finds himself propped up against a tree. The pain throughout his body is terrible but he knows he'll live.

To his right, a few feet away he sees Sadastra. She has her head in her hands and is sobbing.

Hideo: Saman..ah I mean Sadastra, I'm OK. Don't cry.

She stops for a moment and looks at Hideo. Her eyes are beautiful. He has never seen eyes of quite their darkness. And for a moment Hideo's pain disappears.

Sadastra: I'm sorry I lied to you in the Blue Realm. They made me believe that you were some evil monster bent on destroying their whole civilization.

Hideo: Ow! Oh, I'm sorry... I'm no monster. I'm just a high school student who happened to be sitting by a river when the power to open doorways was being passed out.

Sadastra: What?

Hideo: It's a crazy story. Someday when it doesn't hurt so much to feel my own voice vibrate through me, I'll tell you about it.

Sadastra smiles but the concern can still be seen in her lovely eyes.

Hideo: So...uh...any idea where we are? I know that I was pretty weak so I don't think I opened a door to very far away from the scientists.

Sadastra: This place is familiar to me.

Hideo: I'll open a door to the warrior's city.

Hideo concentrates and a yellow ball of light appears. But the door does not open. Finally the door disappears. Hideo is a bit embarrassed but more in pain.

Hideo: Don't worry I ca ahh I can do this.

He concentrates again and another ball of light appears. The characteristic "wheem" sound is heard but it sounds almost doubled for a moment.

Hideo: Let's go Sadastra.

They both step into the door and exit out the other side. The exit is still in Sinder Forest.

Hideo: Oh, I wonder where we are now.

Sadastra: I think I know.

Hideo: You know this forest well.

Sadastra: Not really.

She points due west. About 80 yards away there is a yellow door.

Hideo: Oh no. I can't open another one.

Sadastra: It looks like we're going to walk then.

Hideo nods.

Sadastra: Can you make it?

Hideo: Is the pain that obvious?

Calmar: I will help.

Out of nowhere there is a rather dignified older gentleman. Hideo and Sadastra are startled.

Calmar: Don't be alarmed. I'm a harmless old man who wants to do a little good in his final years.

They look at each other's eyes for a moment. Then they agree.

Calmar: Follow me.

They follow Calmar to a little cave. The cave is very well hidden. There aren't many comforts in this cave but Hideo is glad to rest.

Calmar: Sadastra, relax.

The old man begins cutting up roots.

Sadastra: How do you know my name?

Calmar laughs.

Calmar: Let's just say that I knew your mother.

Sadastra is startled and she looks very defensive.

Sadastra: Who are you?!

Calmar: Don't worry. I'm a friend.

Sadastra looks unsure.

Hideo: What is it, Sadastra?

Sadastra: He is one of the scientists.

Calmar: No, my dear. I was one of them.

Sadastra looks on waiting for the old man to continue. But he doesn't.

Hideo: So, you just live out here by yourself.

Calmar: Yep.

Hideo: That's crazy.

Calmar: I've been called a madman by many. So, I take no offense at your words.

Sadastra: Why did you leave them?

Calmar: I...had some disagreements with them.

He gives Hideo a cup of liquid.

Calmar: Drink this; it will bring some of your strength back.

Hideo: I don't like the way they get things done either. But they don't sound like they're interested in harming others just protecting themselves.

Calmar's eyes flash with anger.

Calmar: They harm everything they touch!

Calmar realizes that his outburst is strange. And calms himself.

Calmar: You just don't know all the things that they've done.

Hideo: They couldn't be as bad as Maubuus.

Calmar laughs.

Calmar: They CREATED Maubuus!

Hideo: What?!

Maubuus' Castle

In front of Maubuus' castle stand 4 cutthroat assassins. Their names are Geleel, Curos, Munoir, and Ag. Each of them has been specially trained by Maubuus for sneak attacks. They are experts in devastation.

All of them except for Curos have been trained since they were babies to want to kill. Although Curos was not trained from the time he was a baby, he has no less of a desire to kill. He is a special case. For he was born of the warrior's people. He never became a warrior even though he has the ability to shine.

Geleel: I feel like a fool following this bird.

Munoir: Disobey Maubuus and you won't have to worry about feeling anything again.

Ag: Look on the bright side, we get to kill!

The assassins smile.

Munoir: Curos, how do you feel about going against your people?

Curos: I don't care about them. Besides if what I've heard is right the Doorway isn't even one of my people!

Munior: Maybe you will hold back.

Curos: I should kill you here.

Munior: Just because you can shine doesn't mean that I won't slit your throat!

The two square off.

Ag: Stop it! I'm the leader here. If you don't stop fighting I will kill both of you. Do either of you doubt my word?

Munior: No.

Curos: No.

Ag: Don't anger me then.

Munior and Curos give each other a very evil look.

Calmar's Cave...

Calmar: What did they tell you about themselves?

Hideo: They said that they were just protecting themselves and protecting this realm. They thought that I was going to introduce foreign weapons, foreign evil into this realm.

Calmar: No. More likely they're worried about losing control here. They're the top here. They're in control and they're worried about another gaining control.

Hideo: They said they could time travel to a certain degree. They discovered that in the not too distant future their whole civilization will be destroyed.

Calmar: For the things they've done, they deserve it.

Hideo can see the hate Calmar has for them. But he can also feel that he is ashamed to have been one of them.

Hideo: They're your people. Do you really want them to die?

Calmar pauses at the question and just thinks for a moment.

Calmar: I ... no. They're just set in their ways. They'll never change. They hide the truth in their search for it.

Hideo: What do you mean?

Calmar: Didn't you notice a snobbishness about them?

Hideo: Yes, definitely. They referred to me...

Calmar: Like you were an animal! That's exactly what they think of you. You're nothing more than animal to them. This whole thing is an experiment and you're part of it now since they let you go.

Hideo: We escaped.

Calmar: You just don't understand. My people live for science. During the beginning of my race we had superstitions and a belief in magic. Then we realized that all of that stuff was just imagination. We got rid of all that nonsense and used the scientific method to discover all we could about our universe. We made many great strides. Then we started to study other universes. We traveled to these places with our Door machines. Different universes... realms could be entered by their use.

Hideo: The machine the warriors have must be one of the Door Machines.

Calmar: The warriors have a door machine? How did they get that?

Hideo: During a fight with Maubuus we stole it from his castle.

Calmar: Maubuus! My God!

Calmar wants to hear more but he sees that Hideo can barely keep his eyes open.

Calmar: You can tell me more when you awaken and I will tell you more.

Later...

Curos: We're getting pretty deep into this forest. And we haven't found them yet.

Ag: Just follow the bird and shut up.

Geleel: We're getting close. I can feel it. It's almost time. You all can have Doorway. I want to kill the woman that's with him. She sounds so small and weak. Kills are the best when your enemy is totally crushed. When you know that they didn't even have a chance!

Ag motions for the assassins to look up ahead.

Ag: There is a cave. The bird stopped in front of that cave.

Geleel: Why is it so hard to see?

Ag: That's where they are! Spread out and approach the cave silently. Keep a look out for traps, others, or anything else that might give us away.

The assassins silently approach the cave unbeknownst to the three inside.

Inside the cave...

Calmar: You two were really exhausted.

Sadastra: Thank you for your kindness to us.

The old man passes out bowls of soup to his guests.

Calmar: Are you feeling better?

Hideo: I still have pain but I feel much more refreshed. And the pain isn't so bad.

Calmar: Good.

Hideo: I want to thank you too.

Calmar: As I told you, I want to do some good in my final years.

Hideo: You are a good man.

Calmar smiles.

Calmar: I have something to show you.

The old man gets up and goes over to a trunk on the far side of the cave.

Calmar: While you were sleep, I found these charts that I want to show you. Remember when I told you that we were interested in magic when our race was young?

Hideo: Yes.

Hideo's curiosity rises.

Calmar: Well, during our explorations we found that other cultures had these beliefs too. These things brought about a kind of nostalgia among my people. We decided to conduct an experiment in this realm. There were various primitive peoples here. The stage of development was perfect. We planned and set the parameters of the experiment. It took a hundred years for us to come up with a method of conducting this that was agreed upon by all.

Hideo: That long?!

Calmar: Yes, every detail was discussed and planned.

Hideo: Wow. How long was this experiment supposed to last?

Calmar: We wanted to follow it for at least 1500 years.

Hideo is flabbergasted at the time scales.

Hideo: How long do you guys live?

Calmar: Oh, about 220 years but that's no obstacle. Our information is just passed along to the younger scientists. I wasn't here when the experiment initially started but once I was chosen to become part of it I studied every detail of it.

Hideo is speechless.

Calmar: It was decided that we would slow if not halt technological progress here because science might hinder their belief in magic.

Hideo: Progress certainly is slow here. How did you stop technology?

Calmar: We couldn't completely stop it. We slowed it down to almost nothing though. We monitored the civilizations and every time a breakthrough was about to happen, we'd arrange for the discoverers to... die.

Hideo: Arrange?

Calmar: Disease, famine, accident... assassination...

Hideo: That's terrible!

Calmar: They were lab rats to us. With no technology they would rely solely on magic and superstition!

Hideo: You would have to do a lot of monitoring to catch every little advance.

Calmar: That's where Maubuus comes in. We needed a greedy tyrant to conquer all these little civilizations so we would have less to monitor. We genetically engineered Maubuus from the blood of many of the natives of this realm.

The old man has made his way back over to Hideo with the charts in his hand.

Calmar: War raged in this realm with the advent of Maubuus.

The little civilizations that weren't completely wiped out joined with Maubuus.

All during this time we noticed that magic seemed to be working here! The studies of magic in our realm all came up fruitless. But here magic worked! It was influencing the way things happened.

Hideo is totally captivated by the story.

Hideo: But all this doesn't explain why you left the scientists. You saw some of this and you had to know some of this before you became a part of this experiment.

Calmar: ...Yes. We discovered 3 things while studying the people here. The 3rd led to a devastating war on my planet and to fighting here too.

Hideo: What were the three things?

Calmar: The first was that magic and ancient practices worked, the second was this.

He hands Hideo the charts. Hideo looks but doesn't quite understand.

Calmar: The chart shows different time periods and the relative power of the warriors as opposed to Maubuus.

Hideo noticed that when Maubuus was strong so were the warriors and when Maubuus was weak so were the warriors. Calmar nods his head as he realizes that Hideo recognizes the correlation.

Calmar: Here Maubuus was at his most powerful. And just after that, the most powerful warrior ever was born, Bolt.

CHAPTER 9

THE FOUR

Calmar: AAA!!!

The assassin Ag has entered the cave undetected and hit Calmar in the head with a boomerang. Calmar falls to the cave floor.

Ag: I've come to kill you Hideo.

Hideo: Who are you?

Ag: Death for you!

He charges Hideo but gets blown out of the cave by a gust of wind. The wind seems to have come from Sadastra.

Hideo: Sadastra...

Hideo looks stunned at Sadastra but then remembers Calmar. He turns to Calmar but Calmar has disappeared. Hideo and Sadastra run outside to fight Ag. Out of nowhere another boomerang comes flying towards Sadastra. It's going to hit her on the side of the head but at the last second she seems to blow apart. The wind actually seemed to blow her apart! Till she disappears. Then it blows her back together a few feet away.

Hideo: Sadastra?

Hideo is so stunned that he almost doesn't see the third boomerang come flying at him. Instinctively he opens a door just in time to save himself.

Hideo: Sadastra, I can shine! Let's get out of here!

Sadastra: Yeah!

Curos: DOORWAY!

Hideo turns and sees Curos. Curos is using the hypnotic eye. He is focusing on Hideo and Sadastra. Hideo feels its power. His mind is put into a sleepy dreamy state akin to the drugs used by the scientists. There is one big difference though. Hideo is completely aware of what's happening. He just can't move his body and he can't look away. He becomes completely focused on Curos. Sadastra again creates a wind to blow Curos down. It knocks him down but is abruptly discontinued as Geleel jumps Sadastra. He picks her up over his head.

Munoir charges Hideo, yelling.

Munoir: I'll kick the life out of you!!

Sadastra sees what is happening out of the corner of her eye. She tries to send a wind that way. It is a bit off target though. It hits Hideo and knocks him to the side just as Munior kicks.

The kick was aimed for Hideo's heart but instead it hits a glancing blow to the side of his chest. It is still enough to knock Hideo backwards and seriously hurt him. With the near death blow a strange thing happens. Doors seem to scatter wildly from Hideo. A myriad of beautiful lights fly out and open in the blink of an eye. The sound of the "wheems" and the flash of the light is dazzling.

Sadastra sees a streak of color as she falls through the air. She crashes into Hideo as he tries to stand. Together, they fall through a multicolored door. The assassins run toward the door.

Sadastra: Close the door! Hideo, close the door!

Hideo is flat on his back. He raises his head and looks at the door. He sees Ag heading towards the door screaming a war yell.

Ag: AAAA!

Hideo: AAAA!

Sadastra: CLOSE THE DOOR!

Hideo: Oh.

Ag jumps toward the open door. But as he reaches it, it is gone.

Hideo falls back on the ground.

Sadastra: Are you ok?

Hideo: I don't think so. I'm really hurt. It hurts when I move much.

Sadastra: Oh, what should I do?!

She cradles Hideo's head in her arms.

Hideo: When I met you, I wished that you would hold me. I guess I got my wish.

Sadastra doesn't have a chance to respond because of the sound of rustling bushes and many feet approaching them.

Sadastra: Don't worry Hideo. I'll protect us.

Suddenly out of the bushes a large blue wolf comes. He is followed by a red, green, yellow, and white wolf and a man. Sadastra is frozen with fear from the great beasts. They charge towards Hideo and Sadastra. They don't attack though; they run around them, careful not hit them.

Sadastra: They weren't interested in us.

Hideo: They were only interested in getting away from whatever it is that's chasing them!

The rustling of the bushes heralds their arrival.

Hideo: I think we're about to find out what would scare a group of large wolves...

Sinder Forest...

Munoir: They got away.

Ag: Shut up.

Geleel: Maubuus will kill us.

Munoir: Maybe we shouldn't return until we find and kill Doorway.

Out of the cave Calmar emerges.

Calmar: I think that you had better leave here!

Munoir: Why aren't you dead old man?!

Geleel: What are you going to do old man?

Calmar pulls out a gun and fires it at a tree. It destroys the tree. The assassins are stunned.

Ag: We apologize old man. We have no quarrel with you.

Calmar: I have one with you!

The assassins turn and walk away.

Calmar: The cowards! Times they are getting strange.

Elsewhere...

Out of the bushes step two men and a woman. They look stunned to see Hideo and Sadastra. Then they completely ignore them and continue to chase the wolves.

A memory immediately overtakes Hideo.

Hideo: Glass?

The woman stops and turns around. The two men she's with stop too when they see that she has.

Glass: Who are you?

Hideo: I'm Hideo. But I'm also Doorway.

Glass: Are you of our people?

Hideo: No we're not. I just kind of got roped into being a Doorway for your people.

Glass: And the girl?

Hideo: She was a member of the scientist's people...

Sadastra: They are not my people!!

Hideo: Her name is Sadastra.

Glass: Who are the scientists?

Hideo: That's a long story.

Glass: You are hurt.

Hideo: Yeah, I'm pretty bad.

Glass: Touch, tend to his wounds.

One of the men approaches Hideo. He is about the same age as Hideo. His hands begin to shine. He touches Hideo's chest. Hideo can feel the healing powers coursing through his body. The feeling is so good that Hideo feels himself almost sucked into the realm of sleep.

Glass: Shift go put together a stretcher of some sort while the girl and me talk.

Shiftblade: I'm heading out now.

Glass turns to Sadastra.

Glass: Who are you?

Sadastra: My name is Sadastra.

Glass: No, girl. Who are you?

Sadastra: What do you mean?

Glass: You could easily be... one of my people. But you say you are not.

Sadastra: I don't want to talk about this.

Touch: Whew! His wounds were deep. I'm exhausted.

Glass: You can rest when we move him to safety.

Touch: Do you know of the rest of the warriors?

Sadastra: I don't know of them well but I know that Arrow, Barrier, Step and Sword are well.

Touch: Is that all?!

Sadastra: Many died at the battle of the fire.

Glass: What do your people know of that battle.

Sadastra: The scientists are not my people! I was kidnapped from my people! Are you happy now! For all I know I could be one of your people!

Glass: No one among my people has been kidnapped since before you were born. ...Let me rephrase my question, what do the scientists know of the battle of the fire?

Sadastra: From what I've heard they know almost nothing! They had an observer there but he got killed before he could finish his report. It was the first time in their long history that that has happened.

The next morning...

Hideo wakes up in another cave.

Hideo: Thank you very much. I feel strong again! That was amazing.

Glass: You were very hurt. Touch focused his power on you most of the night. You wore him out.

Hideo looks to his right and sees that Touch is sound asleep.

Glass: He won't be able to help us today.

Hideo begins to shine. He makes three doors open at once.

Hideo: I really feel good! I can get you home now.

Glass: We can't go yet. We won't go until we save our fellow warrior.

Hideo: Is there some Maubuuslike figure here that has taken someone hostage?

Glass: No. Back during the battle of the fire, I saw something ... I ... somehow Beast's animal projections were ripped ... and he went crazy.

Hideo: You have a warrior who projects light in the form of animals and he created an animal projection that got ripped?

Glass: Yes.

Hideo: How?

Glass: The whole ... uh ... I don't know. Everything seemed to be torn for a second, even the fire and smoke. There was like a nothingness there slashing through things. I don't understand. Beast had projected only one wolf but it went into this area. It was ... it came back as 4 wolves and Beast kind of went crazy. That's about the time doors appeared everywhere! Touch was sticking close to me. He saw everything I did. We watched as Beast followed the pack of wolves through a door. We followed Beast. Later we came to find out that Beast is no longer sane. He thinks that he is a wolf. He is completely a wild animal!

Sadastra and Shiftblade walk into the cave.

Sadastra: Hey everybody we've got some fruit for breakfast!

Glass: We later met up with Shiftblade who also came here. We've been trying to catch Beast ever since. We think that maybe Touch can help him.

Hideo: I had this dream one time ... uh can maybe the hypnotic eye can help him?

Glass: No, the hypnotic eye doesn't work on our people. It's the symbol of our people.

Hideo: It's a symbol of your people.

Glass: How did you know my name?

Hideo: I met you in a ... vision. I had a vision of a battle in Sinder Forest. You were there.

Glass stares at Hideo.

Glass: You are a strange person, Hideo.

Hideo can't help but to laugh at this statement.

Shiftblade: With Hideo here we should be able to capture Beast easily.

Glass: I was thinking just that. Here's my plan...

Maubuus' Castle...

Milstar sits meditating on the birds. He's watching the assassins and listening to their conversations. He's ready to report everything to Maubuus. His concentration is broken by a knock at his chamber door.

Milstar: Enter.

The door opens and in walks one of the guards to Maubuus' chamber.

Guard: I've notified most of the sons of Maubuus and now I've come to notify you that Maubuus is dead.

Elsewhere...

Near a cliff in the middle of nowhere the stage is set for the capture of Beast. Shiftblade and Touch are with Hideo. Glass and Sadastra are a few yards away. They are on the other side of a little lake.

Sadastra: So this is the pond where they come to water.

Glass: Yes.

The grass crunches as two feet come running to the pond. It's Beast. Beast is sniffing in the air like an animal.

Shiftblade: Touch, focus on Beast and ignore the projections. I'll try to handle them.

Glass: Get ready Sadastra.

Sadastra: I'm ready.

Beast looks around nervously. Finally, he relaxes and begins to lap the pond water.

Shiftblade: Go!

Hideo immediately opens a door near Beast. Beast is surprised and hesitates for a moment. It's almost like he remembers. But then Touch and Shiftblade come out. Immediately two wolves appear out of nowhere. Touch manages to jump and grab Beast. Beast shakes him off though.

Beast heads toward the deep grass. That's when Sadastra uses her wind to blow over stacks of rock that they've set up. The rocks fall on the bits of colored light that have the look of glass. On contact these pieces of glass explode.

Beast is frightened and turns back from going into the grass. Immediately two more wolves appear. They viciously snarl and block Touch from getting to Beast while the other two wolves keep Shiftblade at bay. Hideo opens a door beside Glass and Sadastra. It leads to a door that opens behind Beast. Sadastra and Glass come out of it. Beast spins around and his fifth wolf appears. It jumps at Sadastra and Glass jumps at Beast. Both hit their mark.

The wind blows Sadastra and she blows apart. The wind blows her back together near the cliff. The wolf doesn't give up. It sees her blow back together and runs towards her!

Hideo: Sadastra!!

The wolf reaches Sadastra and knocks her down. She hits her head and is dazed. Hideo quickly arrives at her side though. The wolf jumps Hideo. It's about to bite his neck but then it disappears. Glass has subdued Beast. It's over! They've done it.

Sadastra: Thank you Hideo!

She grabs Hideo and hugs him. Hideo isn't ready for Sadastra's weight. Hideo slips and they both fall off the cliff.

Sadastra: AAA!

Hideo: AAA!

Sadastra: Open a door!

Hideo opens a door to the yellow realm. They fall out the door still heading for the ground at high speed.

Sadastra: Hideo!!

Hideo opens another door. This door opens over a lake in Sinder Forest. They fall into the water thankful that they're alive! They swim to the shore and hug.

Sadastra: We did it.

Hideo: For only the second time, I feel like a real hero!

Sadastra: You are a hero, Hideo.

Hideo blushes.

CHAPTER 10

THE ASSASSINS

Hideo: I'll open a door and bring the four warriors to this realm.

Hideo waves his hand and nothing happens. He tries it again and again nothing happens. Sadastra and him look confused at one another.

Hideo concentrates hard and a multicolored ball of light appears. Hideo tries to open it but he can't.

Hideo: I can't do it. I can't open the door! I can open other doors.

Hideo demonstrates by opening and closing many doors.

Hideo: I don't know why I can't open this door. I could open them while I was there.

Sadastra: Maybe the rest of the warriors can help?

Hideo: Yeah, maybe they'll know something. I'll open a door to the warrior's city.

Sadastra: Should we check on Calmar first?

Hideo: Yeah maybe you're right.

Hideo opens a yellow door to Calmar's cave. They peek into the cave and don't see Calmar.

Hideo: Calmar? Calmar?

Hideo calls out but there is no answer.

Sadastra: I hope he's OK.

Hideo: Me too. I think that he probably is.

Sadastra: I guess that we should go back to the warrior's city.

Hideo: Yeah, but first let's walk together a bit.

Sadastra: Why?

Hideo: Because uh... Calmar might be walking near here. If we walk then we might run into him.

Sadastra understands that Hideo wants to be alone with her. And she wants to be with him too so she agrees with a shy smile.

Sadastra: Ok.

They walk together in silence for a few moments. There is an awkward nervousness about the situation but neither of them wants to be anywhere but here.

Hideo: Sadastra?

Sadastra: Yes.

Hideo: Do you really think that I'm a hero?

Sadastra: Yes, of course. You've been saddled with these doorway powers and you've decided to use them to help a people that you don't even belong to! And you saved me from a wolf made of pure light on a cliff in a strange realm! If that's not a hero then I don't know what is.

Hideo: Well, yeah I guess.

She leans over and kisses Hideo on the cheek. Hideo feels like he's in heaven.

Hideo: Sadastra, did I ever tell you about the time I saved Arrow and Barrier from a whole army sent by Maubuus.

Sadastra: No. Did you really do that Hideo?

Hideo: Yeah, I was...

Hideo continues on with his story as Sadastra listens with wide eyes. Unbeknownst to them is that the assassins are watching their movements.

Munoir: It looks like we're going to get a second chance to kill Hideo.

Ag: And this time it's personal! There is no escape for him this time.

Geleel: Now, that we know that this girl also has power we will be ready for her too. They shall not get away.

Curos: Hey, they're getting away!

Hideo and Sadastra are running and laughing. Hideo is chasing Sadastra.

Sadastra: Come on HERO. You should be able to catch a girl!

Hideo: I will.

Hideo immediately opens a yellow door.

Sadastra: No power, Hideo.

Hideo: I don't need them to catch you!

Sadastra: Then why haven't you caught me?

Sadastra is so busy talking that she slips on a little pile of leaves. This gives Hideo enough time to catch up to her. A freak wind blows leaves in his face as he gets to her. He puts up his hands but there are so many.

Hideo: Hey, you said no powers!

Sadastra: Every woman has the right to change her mind.

Her impish laugh makes Hideo determined to get her. He dives and reaches out. He manages to get Sadastra.

Hideo: I still got you!

They laugh uncontrollably like little children.

Suddenly Sadastra just stops laughing.

Hideo: What is it, Sadastra?

Sadastra: Turn around.

Hideo turns to see Ag, Munoir, Curos, and Geleel standing there.

Hideo: Uh oh.

Geleel: It's time to die!

Hideo creates a yellow light -the precursor to an open door. He makes it shine brightly.

Hideo: I'm warning you! I have my full faculties now. I will hurt you unless you go away!

The four laugh.

Hideo: I'm warning you! I'm a powerful warrior!

Hideo quickly opens the yellow door.

Hideo: Through the door Sadastra!

Sadastra and Hideo move for the door. Hideo hesitates in order to let Sadastra through first. The hesitation is all the assassins need to stop Hideo. Geleel throws a boomerang, which forces Hideo to stop short of the door. Ag throws a boomerang too but Hideo opens another yellow door in front of him to block the boomerang. The boomerang goes into the door. The exit point is a door that has just opened in the middle of the assassins. Geleel doesn't escape the boomerang. The assassins scatter. Unfortunately, Curos goes straight to Hideo. Hideo tries to fight but Curos is too fast. He slaps Hideo around brutally. But when everything looks lost Hideo meets the lunge of Curos with a door. Curos can't stop before going through the door. The exit point of this door is about 100 yards over Hideo's head. Curos comes falling out of this door. He falls into another door 50 yards over Hideo's head. This door's exit point is the door that's a 100 yards over Hideo's head. So, once again he falls out of this door and into the one that's 50 yards over Hideo's head. As he continuously falls through these two doors he keeps picking up speed.

The assassins watch dumbfounded. Finally, Ag and Munoir charge. Hideo notices and changes the exit point of the doorway that is 50 yards overhead to a new doorway that opens up just in front of him. All of Curos' vertical momentum is expressed horizontally as he flies out of the door and slams into Ag and Munoir.

The four assassins are stunned and dazed.

Hideo: I'm winning!! I'm beating four of ... I guess Maubuus' men. Well, I guess I'll be going.

Hideo closes all the open doors and opens one beside him leading to the warrior's city.

Hideo: I hope this teaches you not to bother the warriors! Remember that I'm one of them and I can beat you at will!

Curos stands up. He is obviously very dizzy.

Curos: Wait Doorway. I could have been a warrior but I don't think that they're tough. I also don't think that you're so tough.

With only one real assassin left, Hideo decides to take a moment to fight.

Curos begins to shine. Hideo feels a little intimidated but stands firm.

There is a "wheem" sound and a ball of light appears. It's Curos' light. Curos throws the light at Hideo but it misses. It goes to the right of Hideo. Hideo watches it go wide right and hit the ground.

Hideo: You haven't honed your power very well. You missed me by a mile.

Curos: Oh, did I?

Curos waves his hand and the ball of light attaches to Hideo. Hideo immediately tries to remove it but it sticks to his hand. He pulls his hand away and streams of light remain stuck to his fingers. Hideo panics and tries to use his other hand to remove the sticky light.

Again streams of light remain attached to his hand. It's like sticking your hand in gooey dough. But this light is much stickier than any dough ever was. The more Hideo struggles the more entangle he becomes.

As he struggles he hears Curos begin to laugh. Now the other assassins are beginning to recover too. The situation is quickly becoming out of hand. The others are getting up and joining Curos in his laughter. Hideo's heart is beginning to pound.

Suddenly there is a change. The fear and hopelessness suddenly become openness. He feels a strong desire to please. It's stronger than the hypnotic eye but kind of similar to it.

The unattached ends of the streamers of light flow back to Curos. Curos manipulates those streamers. As he manipulates those streamers, Hideo responds. Curos makes Hideo do a little dance. The assassins laugh hysterically.

Geleel: On your knees!

Curos makes Hideo get on his knees and begin to grovel in the dirt.

Ag: Make him eat dirt!

Hideo begins to stuff dirt into his mouth. The laughter again rises. But then it suddenly stops as Arrow walks through the door that is still open. Following Arrow is Sword, Step, Barrier and Sadastra.

Arrow doesn't say a word. He looks at Hideo's blank stare. Then he looks at Curos and the rest of the assassins. Enough is said in the silent glare that Arrow gives Curos. It seemed like the moment would last forever but the silence is broken as Arrow begins to shine. In succession the "wheem" sound is heard as all the warriors begin to shine. Sadastra sees Hideo and immediately begins to cry. Her tears become nothing more than mist as the wind blows her apart.

Arrow fires an arrow and breaks the strands of light that connect Hideo to Curos. Hideo looks up. He is still in some kind of trance-like stupor.

Ag throws a boomerang at Step. Step easily avoids the boomerang and is quickly on step in the air. Ag moves over to meet Step. Ag uses some of his best moves but they are all countered by Step. Ag throws his quickest blows but Step is just too quick for any of them to land. The fight is basically even until Step decides to fight back. He makes a step appear out of nowhere as Ag punches. Ag hits his hand then Step knocks him out.

Geleel attacks Barrier. Barrier isn't as fast as he used to be. But he is a master at the use of his power. He allows Geleel to hit him a couple of times to pump up his confidence. Then Barrier shines. He punches his barrier outwards as Geleel gets too close. This stuns Geleel. Then Barrier knocks him out.

Munoir attacks Sword. Munoir uses his boomerang to sword fight Sword. Again the fight is an even match. Then Sword changes the color of his sword to red -his sharpest sword. With this he slices through Munoir's boomerang. Munoir turns and runs. Sword throws his sword and it stabs Munoir in the leg. Munoir falls to the ground as the sword disappears. Munoir lies on the ground holding his leg. He's unable to stand.

All attention shifts back to Curos. Curos again reattaches the streamers of light to Hideo. This time they're green. Sword walks up to Hideo and cuts the streamers again. Hideo is still under Curos' control though. As Curos moves so does Hideo. In fact Curos makes Hideo take a couple swings at Sword. Hideo misses each time since his movements are too slow to be of use in battle. The other warriors come to Sword's side.

Curos: Look I still control Doorway! You can't change that!

Curos makes Hideo start dancing. Hideo's movements are slow and wild as he dances into the forest away from the warriors.

Arrow: You dirty, no good...

Arrow loads up a white arrow. It is his most powerful. He fires it at Curos. Curos immediately drops his concentration from Hideo who immediately drops to the ground in a clump.

Curos dives to the ground narrowly avoiding the arrow. The arrow hits a tree. The tree immediately turns white and then becomes dust. Curos lashes out with all his might sending many blue streamers at the warriors. The blue streamers are his weakest but he can fire the most of that type. The streamers swim out and latch onto all the warriors. First there is a struggle inside the warriors but then there is only openness and a wish to please their new master - Curos.

Curos: I was born among your number. I was weak. But now I'm an elite assassin for the mighty Maubuus! He will be so pleased when I bring him your head Arrow!

He pulls out one of the boomerangs that he's carrying. He pulls off a cap over one end to expose a knife.

Curos: Kneel to me warriors - your rightful leader!

The warriors fall to the ground blankly staring at Curos. Curos walks toward the warriors ready to cut off their heads. What a prize they will be for Maubuus.

Behind Curos the wind blows together Sadastra. Sheepishly she stands not knowing what to do. Then she sees Hideo. She runs to him and shakes him. But Hideo doesn't respond. He continues to stare off blankly. Desperation fills her heart and she makes the sign of the hypnotic eye. Hideo's attention is now fixed on her. Breathlessly she continues until Hideo pulls away in full control of his senses. He sees that Curos is about to behead Arrow.

Hideo: No!!

Curos turns around shocked. He immediately fires his streamers of light at Hideo. Sadastra uses her wind to blow the streamers away from Hideo and Hideo uses his power to open a red door under Curos' feet. Curos falls through. And just like that it's over.

There is silence as Hideo surveys the strange scene. 4 warriors kneel staring off blankly. Two assassins lay on the ground unconscious. And one other assassin lay conscious but unable to stand.

Hideo: What are we going to do? The hypnotic eye worked on me because I am not one of the warriors' people. It will not work on them.

Sadastra: I don't know. Will the affects wear off?

Hideo: Let's take them back to the city.

Sadastra: What about the assassins?

Hideo: Let's leave them.

Hideo walks over to Munoir.

Hideo: Remember, we could've killed you but we didn't!

Hideo opens a door to the warrior's city. He gently leads the warriors through the door.

Hideo: We'll take them to the priest. Maybe he'll know what to do.

A while later...

Hideo and Sadastra enter the holiest building in the city of the warriors.

Hideo: This isn't quite what I expected from a church.

The building isn't so elaborate. On the walls there are little fingerprints of blood. There are no chairs in this building just mats strewn across the floor. There are clerics scattered about in meditation. Toward the front of the building is a group of children listening to a priest. Hideo recognizes the priest as the same one who presided over the power transfer.

Hideo heads straight for that priest. The warriors trail behind like zombies staring off into nothingness. Hideo motions for them to sit.

The priest sees Hideo coming and stops speaking.

Priest: I would like to introduce you to Doorway.

The kids turn and look starry eyed at Hideo. Their innocent little eyes amaze Hideo. He doesn't know if it is some kind of special empathy or not but Hideo can strongly feel the love coming from them. It's almost overwhelming.

Priest: These are the young warriors. Show Hideo.

The young children begin to shine. Now the feeling is very overwhelming.

Sadastra: Oh, they're darling!

Priest: This is Jin, Crael, Susa, Corinth, Ker, and Herak. They haven't manifested their power yet so they haven't received their special names yet.

The priest shifts his gaze to the children.

Priest: Now go outside and play. I have to talk to Doorway.

The children walk away talking and laughing amongst themselves.

Hideo: Can you help us? I ...

Priest: I know why you've come. You must stay here overnight and your problem will be solved.

Hideo: How do you know? What will you do?

Priest: I don't know. I just trust my feelings.

Hideo: I've been away from home a long time. I'd like to go home tonight. Is it alright for me to go home and leave the warriors here?

Priest: No.

Hideo: Why?

Priest: I don't know. I just feel it.

The priest smiles and walks toward the exit. The meditating priests open their eyes, stand up and also head for the exit.

Hideo: This is such a strange place.

Hours later ...

Hideo: Nothing has happened we've just been sitting in this place for hours and nothing has happened. I should let my parents know that I'm alright.

Sadastra: You'll get to see them.

Hideo: I guess I should try to think about something else ... Sadastra, were your people of the warriors?

Sadastra: I don't know, but you're the second person to ask me that. Why do you think so?

Hideo: Because you have the hypnotic eye power.

Sadastra: You do too.

Hideo: Only because I'm a Doorway. Also, you are immune to the affects of the hypnotic eye. All of the warriors' people are immune to the hypnotic eye. You even have a power like the warriors. You probably should be a warrior! How did you come to be with the scientists?

Sadastra: I don't want to tell you. You will think badly of me.

Sadastra turns away from Hideo.

Hideo: What could be so bad?

Sadastra: I ... I can't tell you.

She begins to gently sob. Hideo grabs her shoulders and gently turns her back around.

Hideo: You can trust me. I would never think badly of you - no matter how you became affiliated with them. I know what kind of person you are now.

Sadastra looks up at Hideo. Hideo feels the warmth from her beautiful eyes. He feels himself moving closer to her as she moves closer to him.

Suddenly, there is a "wheem" sound. All of the warriors begin to shine except for Barrier. Their glow starkly contrasts the darkness of the unlit room. It's mesmerizing.

Arrow: What happened?

Hideo: One of the assassins did something to you so I brought you here!

Arrow: Oh ... Good job Hideo!

Sword: It was Curos!

Hideo: You know him?

Sword: None of us have personally met him before today but we have heard of his ruthlessness in conjunction with Maubuus!

Step: Arrow, Barrier has not recovered.

Arrow rushes over to Barrier. Arrow sees that a streamer of light is still connected to Barrier. It goes into his head through the ear. The concern can clearly be seen in Arrow's eyes. Barrier and Arrow have been friends since they were little kids.

Arrow: CUROS! Only Curos can fix this and he's dead!

Hideo: Uh ... no he's not.

Arrow: You didn't kill him?

Hideo: Kill? No.

Arrow: Well, now I shall! Where is he?

Hideo: Well, I sent him to the red realm.

Step: The place where Maubuus' army was sent! Oh boy Hideo! You sure know how to pick the exciting places!

Arrow: We go first thing in the morning to the Red Realm! So, sleep well warriors.

CHAPTER 11

THE RED REALM ARCHERS

In no time the warriors seem to be asleep.

Hideo: I have to go home for a little while

Hideo silently walks out of the little church. He is met by the ghostly silence of the city.

Hideo: I have to do this first.

He opens a blue door leading to his room. His room feels so comfortable and familiar. He wants to just relax there and sleep. He feels a sadness as he realizes that he may never see this place again. He looks above his bed and sees the unrepaired marks in the wall that the crossbow bolts made. Beside the bed he sees his treasured writings. He feels the sting of tears as his eyes begin to water.

Hideo: No, I'll write a simple note explaining that I'm OK. Then I'll leave.

He pulls a page out of a notebook and begins to write.

Hideo: Dear mom and dad, I hope you aren't too worried about me but I know that you are. I just want to let you know that I'm alright. I'll be gone for a while but I'll come back as soon as I can. I can't explain anymore. But please remember that I love you.

As he finishes writing a tear falls upon the letter. He puts it in the middle of his neatly made up bed.

Hideo: Now, I'll go.

A yellow ball of light appears then fades away. He feels himself drawn to the other rooms of his house. He quietly walks to his little sister's room and peeks in. She looks like a little angel he thinks. He's never realized that he loves her so much. With only the sound of his shadow, he makes his way to his parents' room. He stops at his parents' door and hears the labored turns of a restless sleep.

Hideo: I can't believe I'm doing this.

With that, Hideo returns to the Yellow Realm. Hideo feels anxious but he sleeps surprisingly well.

Next morning ...

Arrow: Ok warriors, we will be heading into an area where we may encounter the archers that Hideo sent to the red realm. Hideo, I want you to try to feel Curos and open a door near him. Do you think you can do that?

Hideo: I don't know. I can open a door but I don't know how close it'll be to Curos.

Sadastra: How many archers did Hideo send to the red realm?

Arrow: That's none of your concern. We'll take care of this. You'll be safe here.

Sadastra: I want to go too.

Arrow: You are not a warrior and you are not even one of my people. You're just an outsider.

Hideo: That's a terrible thing to say! She saved my life more than once! And if it weren't for her we'd all be slaves of Curos.

Arrow: We don't allow outsiders in our group. We'll afford her hospitality but she will not participate in our society!

Hideo: I know that that's the way things have always been here Arrow but now's the time for new thinking!

Arrow: I am the leader! I say the girl stays here!

Hideo: I control the doors. Without me, everybody stays.

Arrow is completely unaccustomed to having his orders debated. In fact, the very first time that his orders got debated was when Hideo first questioned Arrow's plan to fight the archers. He didn't like it then and he certainly doesn't like it now. But he realizes that there is nothing he can do.

Arrow: Do you think that you can lead the warriors? DO YOU! I will grant your request for Sadastra to come this time because I need YOU. The ancestors saw fit to leave the doorway power with you. Don't challenge my authority again Hideo.

Arrow uses strong words but he knows that they are useless with Hideo.

Hideo: You're trying to make me look like the bad guy. But you don't realize that she may even be one of your people! She has the hypnotic eye. She also has a power. Maybe she should be a warrior!

Arrow: She doesn't shine. She isn't one of us. I don't trust her. Now Hideo, open a door.

Hideo flings open a door. The door opens near Curos. In fact the warriors could see him through the door. The warriors rush through the door to face Curos. They come out to see that Curos has his arms and legs tied.

There are 2 archers guarding him. One archer fires an arrow at Sword but Sword knocks it out of the air. The other archer fires his arrow at Step. It hits Step in the foot. Step hops around in pain. The two archers realize that they are sorely outnumbered. They kneel in surrender. Arrow walks up to one of them and fires his arrow at close range, immediately killing the archer. The other cringes as Arrow moves over to him.

Hideo: Arrow, wait! You can't just kill him. He's surrendering!

Arrow: He would've shown us no mercy Hideo. Why should we show him any?

Hideo: Have you ever tried to reason with any of Maubuus' men?

Step: Arrow! Arrow!

Arrow: What is it, Step?

Step: I've decided to change my name to hop.

There are chuckles of laughter as Step somewhat defuses the tense situation with his wacky sense of humor.

Hideo, the archer, and Arrow don't laugh though.

Arrow: I'm sorry Hideo. I just don't trust Maubuus or his men.

Arrow fires his arrow as the archer covers his face. Hideo feels compelled to act. He opens a door in the path of the arrow. The arrow flies through the door and closes it with a bright flash.

Archer: Please...Please... I don't serve Maubuus ... I don't serve Maubuus!

Arrow: What are you doing Hideo?!

Hideo: He says that he doesn't serve Maubuus!

Arrow: He's lying!

Hideo: Maybe he can give us information about Maubuus.

Arrow: He'll lie!

Archer: I'll tell you whatever you want to know.

Hideo: Did you hear that?

Arrow: He lied! Hideo, I know these people better than you.

Archer: What I said was true. None of us want to serve Maubuus! He's cruel. We all fear him!

Arrow: All?

Archer: Yes! We want to be free of him.

Sword: Is that why you tied up Curos?

Everyone glances Curos' way, only to see that Curos is gone.

Hideo: Can you help us get Curos back?

Archer: Yes. There are many of us here. We could help you try and capture him.

Sword: If Maubuus is not your leader now then why did you attack us?

Archer: Because you are not one of us. We fought you in the yellow realm. Why should we assume that you want to be friends just because we are in the red realm?

Sword: Hmmm...

Archer: I'm sure that we could have an alliance now.

Arrow: Again, I don't trust you.

Archer: We don't trust you either. But we prefer you to Maubuus.

Hideo: We need them to find Curos. I opened a door beside him last time but I'm sure you know that that was mainly luck.

Arrow: Let's find cover and we will discuss this. Hop can you keep a look out for us?

Step is limping too badly.

Step: Uh, Sword would you do the honors.

Step creates a series of Steps in the air so that Sword can climb to a height where he can see most of what's going on.

Sword: I see a clearing up ahead. It looks like it would be very hard to get to. So it's perfect for us.

Arrow: Come down here Sword. Sword and I will scout this area out and make sure it's safe. I'm counting on you Hideo to watch the archer and help Step. Can you handle that?

Hideo: Of course.

Arrow and Sword make their way off into the thick brush. Sadastra is tending to Step's foot.

Hideo: So, how's life in the red realm?

Archer: We're making a life for ourselves here. It's a little rough but at least there is no Maubuus.

Hideo: How long has Maubuus been a king?

Archer: Seemingly forever.

Hideo: We've had violent evil dictators in the blue realm too. Take heart, they always die or are either killed.

Archer: I don't think that Maubuus will be doing either.

Hideo: Maubuus is very old but everyone dies.

Archer: Not Maubuus. You don't understand. Years back I was a high guard. That means that I guarded Maubuus' chamber. Some of the things I saw were... my God! If I told someone directly under Maubuus' power I would certainly be killed. But I'll tell you ... Hideo. Some of chamber guards decided to rebel against Maubuus. Maubuus is most vulnerable when he is sleep.

Hideo: Were you among those that rebelled against Maubuus?

Archer: Oh, no. All of those guys are dead. Maubuus killed them.

Hideo's eyes get big.

Archer: They sneaked into his room and stabbed him through the heart. It took all three of the men wielding a solid silver blade to get the blade into Maubuus. But Maubuus didn't die! He opened his eyes and horribly slaughtered the three men. One of their skulls still adorns his bed.

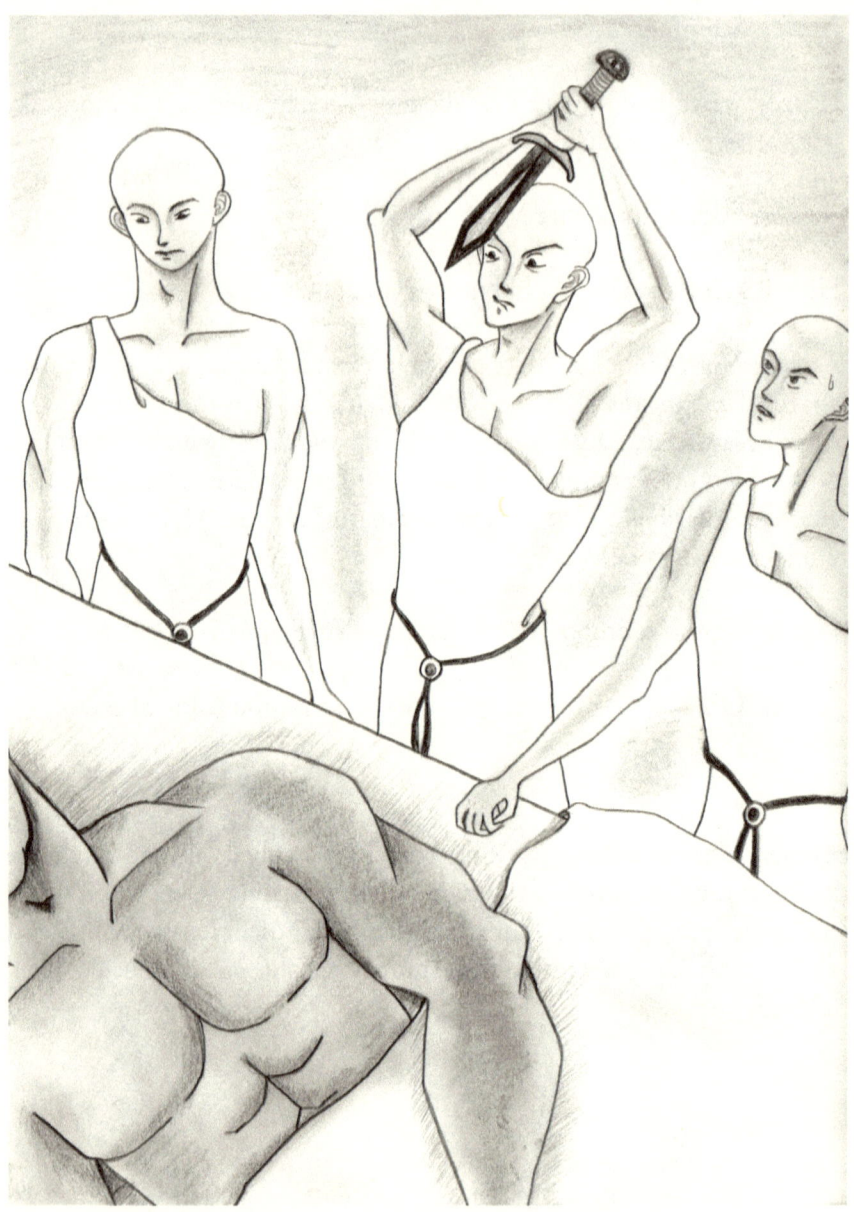

Hideo: How badly did Maubuus bleed?

Archer: He bled profusely. This is where I came in. The off-duty chamber guards had to come to Maubuus' aid. I saw the blood everywhere. Maubuus wailed like a wounded beast. I'll never forget that sound or the blood pouring from his chest. Any man would have died then and there. But ...

Hideo: Maubuus didn't.

Archer: That's right. But a couple days later Maubuus did die.

Hideo: Impossible, I just fought Maubuus a couple of weeks or so ago!

Archer: Let me finish the story. When he died his sons came and collected the corpse.

Hideo: Maubuus must have a lot of children.

Archer: Yes he does ... The heirs of Maubuus held a series of brutal games. Usually the loser of a game would be killed but sometimes one would survive. The ultimate victor would later ritually execute the survivor.

Hideo: Not much reason to survive.

Archer: No.

Hideo: So the winner becomes the new leader.

Archer: You don't quite understand. They were not fighting to become the leader. They were fighting for ownership of Maubuus' body.

Hideo: Why?

Archer: So that they could eat it.

Hideo looks for a sign of laughter from the Archer. -Something to say that the archer is joking. He doesn't find anything.

Hideo: That's ... that's disgusting! Why would they eat their father's corpse?

Archer: I never saw it. But rumor is that their bodies change. They change and become Maubuus. Not just the same body features as Maubuus but Maubuus himself! There are two spirits in one body.

Hideo stares open mouthed.

Hideo: That's impossible.

Archer: All I know is that I saw Maubuus die! And I know he rules now! You tell me what happened!

Hideo is at a loss.

Hideo: How do you know there are two spirits in one body?

Archer: I can't know for sure but I know that somehow the new Maubuus knows everything that the old Maubuus did! I saw some really strange things when I worked as a chamber guard.

Hideo: How did you become an archer for Maubuus?

Archer: After the assassination of Maubuus, I was given my choice of positions since I had helped Maubuus. I chose ...

Sadastra interrupts.

Sadastra: It's Curos!

Curos comes walking out of the forest. He has a black eye. Hideo begins to shine along with Step. Hideo isn't quite sure what he's going to do but he shines brightly anyway. Behind Curos comes Arrow. He's holding an arrow poised to fire in the bow.

Curos: You know if you shoot me, I won't be able to help you with your problem.

Arrow: And what problem is that?

Curos: You tell me. I can't help but notice that I'm still alive. You would've killed me already if you didn't need me. You sure wouldn't have come to the red realm to get me unless you needed me!

Arrow: Don't think that I won't kill you. You're right though I do need you! But if you cross me I'll just make an alternate plan that involves your belated death.

Curos: How do I know that your current plan doesn't involve my death?

Arrow: You don't! Now shut up!

Curos doesn't say anything else but he rolls his eyes.

Sword follows Arrow out of the brush.

Sword: We found him headed in the same direction that we were.

Arrow: We won't be needing the archer anymore. Kill him Sword.

Sword moves over to the archer.

Hideo: Wait we should let him go. We got who we wanted. There's no reason to kill him.

Arrow: No reason?! His people attack mine. His leader wants us dead. They have killed my ancestors and they will kill more of them.

Hideo: He was just ordered to kill by Maubuus. Most of the yellow realm is oppressed by Maubuus.

Arrow: Ok! Ok! Just let him go! Let's get back and help Barrier.

Archer: I won't forget this, Hideo. Maybe we can help each other in the future.

The archer turns and walks into the woods. Hideo opens a door back into the church in the yellow realm.

Arrow: Curos, go through after Sword.

Curos: Hnnh.

The group emerges in the little church where again several priests are meditating.

Curos: Why am I here?

Sword: See Barrier over there? You did that to him and you're going to undo it!

Curos: If I do undo it then you'll no longer need me. You'll certainly kill me.

Arrow: We will let you go.

Curos: I don't trust you!

Sword: Don't trust us?! You're the traitor. We're your people but you fight for Maubuus. You've turned your back on us and on our ancestors.

Curos: You're weak! You're backwards believing in the ancestors. If they were so great they wouldn't be dead! You don't work for yourselves. You work for your people and your ancestors. You'll never truly be great! I work for myself.

The argument goes on without regard for the priests who have begun to chant in unison.

Sword: You serve Maubuus!

Curos: Maubuus gives me my own territory! I rule there!

Sword: You answer to Maubuus.

Curos: I've decided not to help you. You just plain disgust me.

The humming is getting louder and louder.

Curos: I hate you and I hate the ancestors! Look at how easily I play with you.

Curos begins to shine and Barrier stands up and dances.

Barrier: Curos is my king. Curos is my king.

The chanting is very loud. The singing of Barrier is also very loud. The cacophony is joined by Curos' insane laughter, the angry words of the warriors, and the "wheem" sound of the warriors' light. Hideo just watches. Suddenly Barrier begins to shine. And the church seems to be filled with a white light for a moment.

Barrier: AAAAAAA!!!

Jethri: What happened?! This definitely goes into my report.

That ended a very strange month. Barrier was healed and Curos was jailed.

Half a year passed like this. Hideo began to get used to this strange place. Hideo was a hero like in his dreams as he became better and better at using the doors. He became a true asset on the warriors' adventures those 6 months. Things had really changed since Hideo first became Doorway. Things were about to change more than anyone had expected.

CHAPTER 12

THE DATE

The abode of the scientists...

Head scientist: Gentlemen of the council I would like to present to you the findings of our latest jump into the future. The brave Koro made it. May he rest in peace.

The council room dims and a totally immersive virtual reality environ replaces it.

Koro: I've successfully arrived in the future! The time here appears to be about 2 p.m. Our society seems to be basically destroyed. I've come too late in the day. Since this will be our last chance to jump to the future to find out what happened, I'll try to find out as much as I can. I hope you are receiving this information.

Koro begins to look and walk around.

Koro: Over there is where the citadel used to be. I will search the ruins for survivors. If I can just find one then maybe I can find out what happened here.

The fire and smoke are thick but Koro makes his way through it in a very determined way. He is frantically searching.

Koro: No! There are only dead bodies and destruction! I ... I must control myself. I'm a scientist.

Koro continues to frantically run through the city. Suddenly a white static seems to start interfering.

Head scientist: I apologize for the quality of the transmission. We were straining our systems energy wise just to keep Koro in that time.

Councilman 3: Quiet. Let us hear the rest of what happened.

Koro: I hear screa... northwes... I'm ... that way.

The interference was getting more pronounced but still Koro could basically be understood.

Koro: What ... sound? ... the building!

Koro runs to the other side of a building.

Koro: I see ... but ... Hideo!!

Koro falls to the ground.

Head scientist: That was the end of the transmission. When Koro's body reverted back to this time, he was dead.

Councilman 1: Why couldn't we see what he saw on the other side of the building?

Head scientist: Because he didn't come from behind the building enough. The view of the holographic cameras sewn into his uniform were blocked by the building.

Councilman 1: It sounds like Hideo was definitely involved in the demise of our culture. He was there when our people were destroyed! Now it seems that the prudent measure would be to make sure that he isn't able to be here 5 days from now. That means that we will have to take him out before that time. Is it agreed?

Councilman 2: It is agreed.

Councilman 3: It is agreed.

Jethri: I will prepare the hovercraft for the assault. I will bring back a genetic specimen to show that I have killed him.

Councilman 2: There is no need Jethri. Since we will be accompanying you. We will watch him die ourselves.

In another part of the yellow realm the warriors are returning from talks with a people known as the Grell. They are the last independent tribe left on the planet besides the warrior's people. They've been discussing mutual defense plans for the past 3 days.

The talks have taken place at the urging of Hideo. Hideo has weakened the warriors' deep-rooted distrust of outsiders. A new way of thinking that is necessary for survival. These talks would've never taken place without Hideo and without Arrow's new found trust in him.

Sword: The Grell are a good people.

Arrow: They've survived by luck and cunning against the power of Maubuus. They are tired of constantly running from Maubuus. They are now ready to fight for their right to be free.

Barrier: Yes. That is a good thing. Our two peoples together will make it harder for Maubuus.

Step: Making life harder for Maubuus is always the beginning of a good plan for me!

In Sinder Forest at Calmar's Cave...

Calmar has a small device and with it he's watching the hover ships make their way through the forest.

Calmar: Something big is occurring.

Calmar runs over to another device and fiddles with the controls. As he touches the device, he begins to remember another time -the time when he first got this device.

Calmar: Yes, it was a long time ago by the way some folks would count. -A good 20 years ago.

Calmar loses himself in memory of when he was on the council of scientists...

Calmar: I will no longer be a part of the deceit you spread among our people! They must know!

Councilman 2: Why, so that they will destroy this place just as the masses did in our realm?

Calmar: I resign as councilman 1, Enato. Now, all of you can move up! It's what you've wanted.

Councilman 2: No, I've never wanted your position! You're just afraid of responsibility and now you're running.

Calmar: I am the lead councilman but you will not follow my lead!

Councilman 2: You know the last orders of our leaders forbid us from letting the people know! I'm going to follow those orders. And the rest of the council agrees with me!

Calmar: Last orders?! Look our home was destroyed! What gives them the right to give us any last orders? I blame them for all of the destruction and war! And now look what our experiments have done to this realm! I will not be a part of it.

Councilman 2: Then you must die!

Calmar: You are supposedly so civilized. You are so much better than the common animals of this planet but you would just kill me in cold blood.

Councilman 2: You try to paint me as a monster Calmar. We've always been great friends. It's only lately that you've changed. We would not kill you for any reason. You know too much Calmar. We couldn't risk you just being among the general scientists. It would destroy us.

Calmar: Our civilization is already destroyed! Look at the Green Realm! It's a wasteland! Now we're falling apart here. You can't keep your secrets anymore. Whether it be today, tomorrow, or 50 years from now our civilization will fall!! It will fall because of our inability to adapt and accept new ideas! That is the core upon which we have grown.

Councilman 2: You are hereby stripped of your role as lead councilman. Guards take him away to await his death.

Calmar comes out his daze of memory with a stony frown on his face. He slowly becomes aware of the sound the device he is holding is making. There are voices coming from it. The voices are those of the councilmen.

Councilman 1: We must destroy Hideo as soon as possible.

Guard: Sir what if we get resistance from the warriors?

Councilman 1: They will have to be eliminated then. This is war!

Calmar throws the device to the ground!

Calmar: Enato you are a fool!! I will not let you destroy more people. I couldn't stop you before but now I ...

Calmar again slips into memory, harsh memories. -Memories of being in a holding cell awaiting his death. He waited there for hours. The scientists hadn't anticipated the rebellion happening that very day. The scientists who knew the real reason that the Green Realm Armageddon occurred fought for their autonomy. A brilliant scientist named Vlad led them. He had done most of the genetic engineering on Maubuus. Some say that he was a little insane.

Calmar remembers seeing the chaos. He also remembers hearing of the horrific battle that killed all of the rebels. The battle was known as the Battle of Sinder Forest.

Calmar: I'm going to stop this!

The old man heads out of the cave.

Back with the warriors…

Barrier: I didn't like their food very much.

Sadastra: It wasn't that bad.

Step: What's that sound?

Step climbs into the air for a better view.

Step: Uh oh Arrow! I think that we could have trouble.

An instant later 10 hoverships are just there floating in the air. Each ship holds 3 soldiers. The warriors look on unsure whether this is an enemy or a friend. They soon find out as the ship that has councilman 1 speaks out.

Councilman 1: You will give us Hideo. You are outmanned and vastly overpowered. You will be destroyed unless you do what we say. What is your reply?

Arrow: Warriors!

Maubuus' Castle...

No one realizes the new plan that Maubuus is about to unleash on the warriors. One so diabolical only Maubuus could've thought of it.

Maubuus: For a long time the warriors have been a problem for me. The warriors put a good portion of my men in the red realm using the door I procured so long ago. They took the door so now I can't retrieve my men from the red realm! They thought they were so smart but now they will pay.

Milstar: My birds have noticed that the warriors are now returning to their beloved city.

Maubuus: Won't they be surprised. They are too foolish to realize that the doorway machine is missing its remote activator! How else can one return from a realm once a door has timed out! The door is in the middle of their city! Yes the time is ripe. The date of my revenge is approaching.

Back with the warriors...

Hideo stands in the middle of a circle of warriors. Arrow stands at the front of the circle. Sword and Barrier stand to the left and right of Hideo. Step is a little bit above the group. And Sadastra is behind Hideo. Arrow fires an arrow at the lead hovership. The arrow hits an invisible barrier of energy before it reaches the ship. The arrow lights up the barrier but it is otherwise unaffected.

The lead ship then fires at Arrow. Arrow gets off another arrow just before the beam hits him. There is a great explosion, as the beam and the arrow meet, which blows Arrow backwards. And knocks the warriors down. Step stands above it all watching.

Sword: Oh that hurt!

Sword throws his sword at one of the hoverships. Again the energy barrier lights up. When the flash goes away, Step is staring at the hovership occupants with the hypnotic eye! All three of the scientists begin to succumb to Step's power.

Councilman 3: Stop him!

Several ships open fire. Hideo immediately opens a few doors so that Step will not be hit. So more ships fire until they overwhelm Hideo's ability. Step doesn't get hit though. He jumps off of his step of light.

Arrow is only partially conscious. He can see what is happening but he is not able to act.

The Warriors City...

Near the center of the warrior's city is a small stone building. It's not particularly adorned but one will notice that the windows have stone bars built into the windows. These bars keep prisoners from escaping because this is the jail. There are only 5 inhabitants of this place. None of them are particularly noteworthy except for one. He is a man that the other inmates consider insane. They think him so because he talks to birds and thinks that they can understand him. His name is Curos.

Inmate 3: Hey Curos! Is your bird going to get you out today?

Curos: Don't forget that I'm an assassin of the mighty Maubuus. When I get out, you will be one of the first ones that I kill.

Inmate 3: Ooh! Is that a promise or a threat?

Curos: It's both!

Inmate 3: Oh, I guess I should really be scared ... once your bird lets you out! Ah ha ha ...

The whole building breaks out in laughter. Curos can feel the heat of anger filling his head. He's being laughed at! No one has ever shown such disrespect for Curos and not been killed.

Curos: You'll soon get YOURS! AHHAH!! SHUT UP! SHUT UP!

The other inmates delight in Curos' pain.

Inmate 2: Hey look the bird is back!

A little blue bird alights on the window. Curos runs over to the window and grabs the bird.

Curos: Get me out of here Milstar!!

Inmate 3: Oh, please don't mr. bird. He'll kill me!!

The inmates again laugh.

Curos: Everything is set. They've left the doorway machine outside for the past 3 days. I can see it from my cell. Now get me out of here!!

The inmates laugh. And far away Maubuus laughs too. Of course, he doesn't care about Curos but he does delight in his plan.

Maubuus: Hideo is so smart! He noticed that the machine had solar cells on it. He knew the machine didn't have any energy so he got the warriors to take it outside!!! Now he has given me a door into the very heart of their city! HA HA HA HA!!!

There is no laughter with the warriors. They are embroiled in a life or death battle with the scientists.

Councilman 3: It's Hideo that we want! Focus on Hideo! All ships open fire!

All of the ships shoot blazing light at Hideo. Hideo is frozen with fear. Luckily Barrier isn't. Barrier steps in front of the coming rays and puts the Blue Barrier around himself. The blue barrier is Barrier's strongest. The beams hit the barrier and immediately knock it off. Barrier falls to his knees. He's saved Hideo but it has taken all his strength.

Sadastra is blowing as hard as she can but nothing is happening. The wind is only hitting the shields of the hoverships.

Councilman 1: Fire again! This time we have him.

The ships again fire their deadly beams at Hideo. Hideo opens doors to block the beams but the beams keep coming. Sadastra sees the predicament that Hideo is in.

Sadastra: Hideo!!

She uses her power to blow Hideo to another place. Unfortunately, a beam grazes Hideo. The slight touch blows Hideo backwards. Had it been a little closer it would've killed him. The reaction is so violent though that it rips the doors from Hideo. Millions of doors open up. The beautiful colored ovals seem like they are everywhere. Sadastra runs to Hideo and again cradles him.

Hideo: Sadastra, I love you.

Sadastra: Get up Hideo! Get up.

Hideo: I can't I'm too hurt. It's over for me.

Sadastra: No, Hideo. Don't give up!

Hideo: I love you, Sadastra.

Sadastra: I love you too.

Councilman 3: One last shot!

Somehow Arrow has gotten to his feet.

Arrow: You will die! WARRIORS!!

"Warriors" is the rallying cry that Arrow always uses. It doesn't seem to work this time. Barrier lays with almost no strength, Hideo lays seriously injured, Sadastra holds him heartbroken, and Step and Sword are also incapacitated. It seems like his cry is completely ignored. But in fact it isn't. His voice carries through the open doors. It's heard by Glass, Beast, Shiftblade and Touch.

CHAPTER 13

THE YOUNG WARRIORS

Arrow: I don't know why you are doing this but you will pay!

Councilman 2: If you had just handed Hideo over to us then none of you would've gotten hurt.

The councilman gives the nod for one of the ships to fire. The guard on the ship presses the fire button. As the energy pulses out of the hovership's laser canon the guard catches a glimpse of light being reflected as if there was a pane of glass sitting in mid-air. He wonders why.

The energy strikes the explosive glassy light of Glass creating an horrendous explosion. -An explosion that causes explosions on many of the hoverships. One after another the tightly clustered ships explode or crash. It is obvious that scientists are not experts of war. Clustering the ships so closely together was foolish and now many of them are destroyed. The two that manage to crash explode on the ground. 27 of the scientists and 3 councilmen came to fight and now 15 of those scientists are dead. Four of the survivors are completely incapacitated. And three of the remaining 8 have fled. 3 injured councilmen and 5 injured scientists stagger amongst the smoke and destruction.

Councilman 3: Attack the war..cough...cough...warriors!

Five wolfen beasts of light have made their way into the area of the downed ships and are attacking the weary guards. The screams are heard among the thick smoke. Touch has made his way to Hideo and is extending an orange light to Hideo. Both are engulfed in the orange light.

Sadastra: Touch, what are you doing?

Touch: We are sharing my life force so that he can heal.

Hideo stands.

Hideo: It's OK Sadastra.

All of the warriors make their way up and slide into a circle around the orange light of Hideo and Touch. The doors close and swirl around once as balls of light. Then they all combine back into Hideo.

Councilman 3: Now hold on for a second.

Arrow doesn't listen. He kills councilman 3. The other two councilmen fall to their knees.

Hideo: No don't. They wanted me. Let's find out why.

Arrow nods in agreement. Hideo steps forward with Touch close at his side.

Hideo: Why are you after me?

Councilman 2: We know that you will be involved in the destruction of our civilization.

Hideo: Why now? When I escaped from you 6 months ago you could have attacked again and had gotten me. But you didn't. You've left me alone for 7 months. So again I ask, why now?

Councilman 2: Do you remember everything from your captivity with us?

Hideo: Well somewhat.

Councilman 2: Do you remember us talking about there being a certain date at which time we would have produced enough energy to travel to the future for a short period of time.

Step: Travel to the future? Sounds like he's been traveling to the wine.

Sword: He's just flat lying!

Arrow: What do you think, Hideo?

Hideo notices how Arrow trusts him now. The past 6 months have brought them closer together. They still have strong arguments concerning Sadastra. Arrow hates the fact that she comes along with them.

Hideo: I think that what he is saying is possible. We still can't do it in my realm but it is being studied.

Councilman 2: We saw you at the destruction of our city! You are part of the destruction of our city.

Hideo: What? Are you sure it was me? What was I doing?

Councilman 2: Well, we didn't actually see you. But the one we sent to the future saw you. He mentioned you by name.

Hideo: I don't want to destroy your culture. I want to protect the warrior's culture.

Councilman 2: I want to protect our culture.

With that the two men stare in silence. No one has noticed that one of the guards that ran away has radioed for help. Now 5 more hoverships arrive on the scene. The tension grows. The warriors are in their circle and the hoverships are poised to fire. The tension is broken by a lone voice crying out.

Calmar: Look at this! Look at all the destruction! Enato! Will you let this continue!

Councilman 1: Calmar?

Calmar: I see that you took my job.

Councilman 1: Stay out of this Calmar! You don't know what's going on.

Calmar: Oh, I know what's going on. You found out that your civilization is going to be destroyed in a few days and you're worried that it's by this young boy!

Councilman 1: Who else could it be? Maubuus is not strong enough, the warriors are not strong enough, and the other tribe on this planet doesn't have any real power at all! An outsider bringing in outside forces is the one plausible solution! His power even allows him to bring great numbers of people from one place to another.

Calmar: You fool! There is one group that you haven't accounted for. You always did leave key elements out of your calculations.

Councilman 1: What are you talking about?

Calmar: I'm talking about the one group on this planet that does have the power to destroy our people. They have a fair amount of technology; they're controlling and power hungry.

Councilman 1: Whom do you speak of?

Calmar: Ourselves!!

Councilman 2: What?

Calmar: We are the only choice. We are the only ones here who can destroy ourselves. It happened in our realm and it can happen here too! We are so busy looking outside for enemies that we don't notice the damage we do to ourselves!

The councilmen never considered these things.

Calmar: Even though there was a civil war just 20 years ago, you are too blind and arrogant to believe that it could be us.

Councilman 1: I ... I don't know what to say. Calmar, I am a fool.

Calmar: Let's let the secret out then. Let's discuss things amongst our people. Our civilization is based on rationale. If we let our people know the truth then there can be discussion. Discussion may avert our destruction.

Councilman 1: Or it may cause it! In our realm the truth got out and our people destroyed themselves. The truth got out here too and directly led to our civil war.

Calmar: The truth was leaked out in both situations. Some believed it and some didn't. The ones who believed it fought to change our policies. They fought against the rigid old thinkers.

Hideo: Was there a nuclear war in your realm?

Calmar: Nuclear weapons were used but these were just toys compared to some of the weapons that were used. We had weapons that you couldn't begin to understand. One of the most devastating was the Temporal Bio-genetic Bomb. The Green Realm was a technological paradise. Now, it's ... it's a shame!

Hideo: What is this horrendous secret?!

Calmar looks over at Enato. Enato nods his head.

Councilman 1: We will try it your way.

Everyone silently listens to Calmar.

Calmar: My people came to this realm to study magic. We were advanced in science and romanticized magic. So we set up an experiment here. To our surprise we proved that magic existed and worked here. The findings were disputed but the inevitable conclusion was that it worked here. Covertly we sought for reasons why it worked. In our history magic never worked. There were always con men that wanted to take advantage of situations and used claims of magic for their own gains. This is all magic amounted to in our history.

Hideo: How does this lead to war?

Calmar: We found out why it worked. We noticed that whenever the warriors were in danger very great heroes were born to them. This wasn't a case of circumstances making heroes. During periods of hardship, they had children with markedly greater - deadlier power! When the times were good the powers were not so strong. The pattern was undeniable. We finally realized that they were somehow receiving help from their dead ancestors. A lot of their rituals and traditions worked because of a little helping hand from their ancestors.

Hideo: But how does this ...

Calmar: I'm getting there. We had been studying the sudden appearance of warriors with powers. We had unsuccessfully probed and studied their bodies for a reason that they had power. Finally we realized that their powers didn't come from their bodies or their blood. It seemed that there was some energy inside of them. -Some natural energy that we couldn't explain. Once we figured out the thing about the ancestors we realized that these creatures had souls. Their souls did not die even though the body did. These souls were the ancestors and they were playing a role in everything!

The guards look on dumbfounded. There is strong sadness in their eyes.

Hideo: I don't understand! Why would your race destroy themselves because of this?

Calmar: Don't you see? Magic never worked for us!

Hideo and the warriors still looked confused. All the guards understand though.

Calmar: The meaning is that we don't have souls! When we die we don't continue on. We were so arrogant. We thought ourselves so much better than the animal races of the other realms. We almost believed ourselves gods! Now suddenly we find out that we are the animals! These little superstitious races that we've been studying are actually better than us.

Again there is silence as everyone digests what has just been said.

Councilman 1: Only the council and a few of the top scientists in this realm knew the complete truth.

Hideo: Oh.

In The City of Warriors

The doorway machine sits out in the open. It is gathering up the warm rays of the sun. The rectangular doorway shaped part of the machine begins to glow green then it changes to yellow. Suddenly through the door come 50 guards of Maubuus! They swarm out of the door and immediately fan out. The people scatter as screams are heard everywhere. The guards go around creating general mayhem.

Five of the guards head straight for the jail. They easily overpower the jail guards. The next thing that they do is free Curos.

Curos: Looks like I'm not so crazy after all! Now you're going to pay!

Curos points to a particular prisoner.

Curos: Give me the key to that prisoner's cell.

Guard 1: Sir, we really should hit our target. The policing forces here will begin to turn us back soon.

Curos: Quiet! I know what I'm doing.

Curos takes the key and opens the cell door. The inmate feels fear as he looks into the insane eyes of Curos. The two fight. Curos viciously beats the inmate. When Curos leaves the cell there is blood everywhere and the inmate is dead.

Guard: Sir we have to hurry.

With only a smile Curos runs with the guards. Together they head for the true goal of their diabolical mission. -A mission straight from the throne of Maubuus. Curos and the guards run through the town headed for one building in particular. The building is the main church of the town. At a certain time everyday all the young warriors come to learn the lessons of their ancestors. The guards and Curos burst into the church.

Curos: Kill everything in here!

Priest: This is a holy place! You cannot be here. You must leave!

Curos: You're going to die!

Curos beats the priest around. Then he throws the priest through a window. Somehow the priest survives but is knocked out.

Next Curos and the guards begin killing the young warriors. Curos doesn't know why but he has always enjoyed killing children. Curos has been on many missions for Maubuus but these are always the best. The priests and the children are slaughtered. The cries of the children echo off the walls. The walls absorb the overwhelming sadness. They are brutally slaughtered.

Curos: Ah, I'm starting to feel like my old self again. Let's get back to the door! Our job's done.

The guards and Curos head again for the exit. The first two are met by the swords of the policing forces. The policing forces charge for the remaining three guards and Curos.

Curos: Get them!

The three guards charge the overwhelming numbers of the police forces. Curos doesn't. He turns and jumps through the window that he threw the priest out of. The exhilaration of the moment fills the body of Curos. He makes his way for the doorway machine.

He jumps over the bodies of the people and the guards. The giddiness of a kid seems to fill him. Curos is as twisted as Maubuus. Curos and about six guards make it to the doorway machine where a little bird is sitting.

Curos: We're ready Milstar.

A button is pressed back at Maubuus' castle. The door machine begins to glow green then it changes to yellow.

Curos is the first through the door. The other six get through the door just before the priest and the police force get to the Machine. The machine shuts off as they stand there looking fearful.

Priest: Get this thing out of the town and throw it in the ocean!

The police scurry to enact the wish of the priest.

Meanwhile....

Hideo: We have to go home!

Arrow: Why?

Hideo: I.. I don't know.

Calmar has joined the scientists and is being welcomed back to them. Calmar suddenly turns to the warriors.

Calmar: Hideo, the warrior city is being attacked.

Arrow: What? Open a door Hideo.

Hideo: Already done.

The warriors run through the door.

Calmar: Wait for me, Hideo! I will help. Come along councilmen.

The scene on the other side of the door is a sad one. Dead bodies are being moved out of the heart of the city.

Sword: Maubuus' blood is as cold as winter on Mount Vander.

Arrow is silent as he surveys the death and destruction. Hideo can see that even Arrow is shaken. Barrier suddenly starts running.

Barrier: Syl! No Syl!

Hideo: Syl? Barrier's wife! Oh my God.

Step: This is the first time Maubuus' men have ever entered a warrior city.

Calmar: Look at what we've done. We're responsible for this.

The other two councilmen are silent. In the distance the priest waves for the warriors to come.

Priest: Look what they've done! They've desecrated the church. Arrow look!

Arrow: Something will be done.

Priest: Come inside and see what other atrocity they've committed!

The warriors and the councilmen follow the priest into the church. There they see the other dead priests and the slain children warriors.

Priest: They killed the other priests and all the young warriors!

Shiftblade: This can't be true! My son!

Shiftblade runs over to one of the dead bodies. He falls to his knees and begins to cry.

Touch and Hideo still share an orange shine. They suddenly begin to speak in tandem with the voices of children.

Hideo/Touch: Please don't kill us! AAAA! AAAA! NOO! Help us! AAA!

Then another strange thing happens. Doors begin to spontaneously open and close. The doors show the young warriors being killed by Maubuus' men.

Arrow: CUROS!!

Emotion fills the little church. The councilmen are touched –watching the heartless murder of the children and the priests.

Calmar: Maubuus is a potato that we added to this stew. We can't let this stand. These people are not animals. Maubuus must be removed. Enato what do you say?

Councilman1: I ... I...

Calmar: Don't be afraid to admit our wrong! Stand Enato! Lead!

Councilman1: You're right.

Enato and Calmar hug.

They were good friends in their much younger days.

Calmar: I always say that I want to do something good in my final years. Let's be a force to right the wrongs we've done together.

Hideo: Arrow, I think we just made a very powerful ally.

CHAPTER 14

THE ALLIANCE

Big changes are coming. The feeling is in the air. Two very powerful forces have joined against Maubuus. Maubuus is oblivious to the plans that seem to be coming together. He sits on his throne surrounded by beautiful women flattering him.

In the middle of the throne room stands another familiar figure. It's Jethri. He is electronically masked from view as always. He stands there observing the behavior of Maubuus. He's logging the last moments of Maubuus.

Jethri: He's just sitting on his throne. I'll just shoot him after I make some final notes.

It's the way of the scientists. All through this planet's history when they wanted to get rid of someone they would just send one of their people to kill them. Usually they would make it look like an accident but this time no elaborate plan is made. Jethri prepares for a routine kill. He's done this a thousand times. But somehow this is special. -The end of an era. -The end of Maubuus.

Jethri walks up to the throne. He places his gun on kill. He then puts the gun near Maubuus' head.

Jethri: Goodbye Maubuus.

Maubuus reaches out and slaps the gun out of Jethri's hand. He then grabs Jethri and pulls his head off of his neck. He throws the head against the castle wall. It splatters as the women scream. The screams mix with Maubuus' laughter. Maubuus crushes the communicator that Jethri was using.

Maubuus: Goodbye Jethri. It looks like the scientists are coming for me. They will find me here. They think that after 3000 years I haven't figured everything out! What fools they are. Especially when they are within my visual spectrum. I didn't plan to fight them this early but they will find that I am prepared. They failed to hide things from me but I do not fail. I will rule the entire realm!! I AM MAUBUUS!!

Later...

Calmar: There is no word from Jethri.

Arrow: So, we are not sure that Maubuus is dead or not.

Calmar: Sadly no. There is even a chance that Jethri is dead.

Arrow: So, we may have to go and take Maubuus out ourselves.

Hideo: From what I was told we would have to go and take him out anyway.

Arrow: The story that the red realm archer told you is pretty far fetched.

Hideo: But even if Maubuus were killed one of his sons would assume the throne. They're probably just as bad as he is.

Barrier: That's true.

Arrow: I agree.

Hideo: Could you tell us more about Maubuus?

Calmar: I'll tell you all that I know. We created Maubuus to bring order to this realm. He was genetically designed with aggressive controlling tendencies. He was also designed with durability in mind. The DNA we used was a combination of many of the creatures ... I mean people that reside in this realm.

Hideo: Could a story like the archer from the red realm told me be true.

Councilman 1: Maubuus wasn't supposed to live as long as he has. And we've never witnessed his death or ... re-emergence. But we have witnessed bloody competitions between his sons. The competitions always end with deaths of ... we think all the sons except one. These competitions are irregular in nature so we don't know much about them.

Hideo: Was he created with a genetic ability to...

Calmar: We really can't say all the abilities that Maubuus was created with. He was created almost exclusively by a scientist named Vlad. He was a little crazy but he was a genius. He was such a genius that we didn't always follow our own rules when it came to him.

Enato takes out a little hand-held device with a view screen.

Councilman 1: This interfaces with our database. This is the meeting where most of the specifications for Maubuus were drawn up. And here is a list of the original specifications. Would you care to read through them?

Hideo: I don't know how much help this would be for me. I probably won't be able to understand most of it.

Hideo takes the little device and flicks through the pages. He flicks to a picture that seems familiar.

Hideo: Who is this?

Calmar: That's Vlad.

Hideo: I've seen him before.

Calmar: Impossible. He died before you came. He led a rebellion about 20 years ago. We found his body where the rebels were stopped.

Hideo: That's it! He was helping Maubuus.

Councilman 1: What?

Hideo: Yeah, and Maubuus killed him. I saw it all.

Calmar: Saw it?

Hideo: It's hard to explain but I saw it.

Councilman 1: So it's possible that Maubuus has technology - if Vlad was helping him.

Calmar: It's obvious that Maubuus has technology. He had a doorway machine.

Councilman 1: What?!

Calmar: That's where the warriors got the one they had. They've dumped it in the ocean.

Councilman 1: This situation just got dangerous. We need to muster all the force that we have to make sure he doesn't have more power than we do!

Calmar: According to the jumps to the future our civilization is destroyed in four days. I suggest we defeat Maubuus before that date arrives.

Arrow: Step, Hideo, and Sword go to the red realm and try to get the archers to help us.

Sword: We'll do our best.

Sadastra brings over some drinks. Arrow rudely brushes her off.

Hideo: I still don't understand why Arrow will still not accept Sadastra.

Barrier: Hideo look at her.

Hideo: What?

Barrier: Don't you think that she looks like Arrow's mother? You saw his mother when you witnessed the past.

Hideo: ... I never noticed. That's impossible though.

Barrier: She couldn't be his mother but just who is she? She's never told us her story.

Step: We should hurry.

Hideo opens a red realm door. Calmar, Sword, and Step go through it.

Hideo: Come on with me Sadastra.

Hideo and Sadastra step through the door next.

Step: OK, now how do we contact the archers?

Hideo: I don't think that is going to be too hard. Just get high and look for the nearest group of archers.

Step climbs high. Almost immediately there's a flurry of arrows heading for him. Step immediately jumps off of his step and falls down.

Step: Well, that wasn't hard.

Sword: They're on their way.

Sword begins to shine.

Hideo: We can't look aggressive. Don't shine. We should raise our hands over our heads.

The four raise their hands over their heads and wait for the archers. The archers come out of the forest with their bows and arrows raised. They look on baffled. They're not quite sure what to do.

Hideo: Please we mean you no harm.

The archers cautiously move forward and begin to tie the warriors up.

Hideo: Please take us to your leaders. We'd like to propose an alliance.

Merl: My name is Merl. I lead this group. Your people were fools to come here! We don't want to be your allies. In fact, we're going to kill you.

Hideo: Wait! Don't you want to go home? Is life so good here?

Merl: Shut up.

Hideo: No! You have nothing here. Your relatives are all in another realm. Your friends are there. I can take you to them.

Merl: You're the one that banished us here.

Hideo: I'll take you back.

Sword: Do not talk to them. They are cowards.

Merl: What did you call me?

Sword: I called you a coward! You'd rather hide in another realm than to fight for the freedom of your people. Your people were free until Maubuus subjugated them.

Merl: I'll kill you first!

Sword: You'll still be a coward. And your people still won't be free.

Merl: Joining with you won't free our people.

Sword: We are going to fight Maubuus. Well we were but I guess we're going to die now.

Merl: Don't lie to me.

Sword: Why would we just come here? We didn't come to just surrender. We came looking for brave men to join our quest.

Merl: Go get the leaders.

He motions to one of his archers. He runs into the forest.

Merl: You will wait here.

Hideo: That was great Sword.

Sword: You have to know how to handle this group. We still don't know what they're going to do though. They could turn on us.

Sadastra is sitting next to Hideo.

Hideo: Sadastra, we may not make it out of this.

Sadastra: Don't worry Hideo. I can free myself anytime I wish. All of us can.

Hideo: Sadastra, please tell me about yourself.

Sadastra: What do you mean?

Hideo: You know what I mean.

Sadastra: Oh. Don't you trust me Hideo?

Hideo: I trust you but do you trust me?

Sadastra: Will you still love me?

Hideo: Forever.

Sadastra: I think that I am a nothing more than a ... a ... oh Hideo! I'm a genetic experiment! I was created by the scientists.

Hideo: Why?

Sadastra: I think they were studying the power of the warriors. I was a cell taken from one of their people.

Hideo: I think I know which one.

Sadastra: Calmar said that he knew my mother.

Hideo: Calmar, did you know her mother?

Calmar: Yes. She was my only friend while I was imprisoned. The scientists found her just after the battle of Sinder. She was wandering aimlessly in the forest. She told me that her husband died.

Hideo: She was the wife of Bolt. Sadastra is a genetically enhanced clone of Arrow's mother. The scientists must've been trying to recreate a warrior power through the blood.

Calmar: They could never get the shine though, because the power had to do with the soul and not with the blood.

Sadastra: I know that I'm just some genetic freak! Sniff sniff.

Sadastra begins to gently cry.

Calmar: You may be a clone but you are still a person. It's the ... the ... soul that makes a person...

Calmar looks off sadly. Just then an army of archers come out of the forest.

Hideo: Wow. Did I send all these people here? Wow.

Sadastra: Wow, Hideo.

Then group parts and out of the forest comes a highly decorated archer. He is larger than the archers and his eyes are sharp.

Shazal: I am Shazal. I rule the archers. I recognize you. You opened the red door!

Hideo: Uh oh.

Shazal: Thank you for our freedom. We are at your service.

Hideo notices that at his side is the archer that he had talked Arrow out of killing. He smiles at Hideo.

Shazal: What is it that you wish?

Hideo: We want to overthrow Maubuus.

Shazal raises his eyebrow.

Back with the scientists, the councilmen, Arrow, and Barrier prepare the final plans for a full assault on Maubuus and His castle.

Councilman 1: It's time to go to the hoverships.

Arrow: Everything is being done so quickly.

Councilman 1: We have to. We want Maubuus destroyed before the date we saw our civilization destroyed. By destroying Maubuus maybe we can avert the destruction of our people!

Arrow: I understand.

They all go to hoverships.

Councilman 1: These are our final 20 hoverships.

Arrow: You should have more.

Councilman 1: This was not a war expedition. And we are not warriors. We don't have heavy weapons. It's time to move out.

Barrier: Aren't we going to wait for Hideo and Calmar?

Councilman 1: There's no time. We're going to make our move.

The army moves on Maubuus' castle. They move quickly to Maubuus' castle.

Arrow: There were no military men blocking us from coming up to Maubuus' castle.

Councilman 2: Maybe we just got lucky.

Arrow: I am a warrior. This is a trap! Keep your eyes open.

Councilman 2: Well let's take the castle. Open fire!

The ships open fire but the lasers do not harm the castle. They hit an energy field that seems to be surrounding it.

On one of the towers, Maubuus steps out.

Glass: Look! It's Maubuus!

Councilman 2: Those poles on top of the castle are generating the field around the castle. Near the ground should accessible.

Arrow: This means that he was expecting you guys. And he knew that you would use hoverships!

Councilman 1: Spread the ships out and get low - very low.

The hoverships go low to the ground and start firing. They are doing damage to the castle.

Councilman 2: ALRIGHT!!

Maubuus: NOW!!

An army comes up from under the sand and begins to jump onto the hoverships. Their numbers are starting to overwhelm the scientists. Maubuus' men are much better fighters. The warriors are holding their own but they too are succumbing to numbers.

Maubuus: Ah, some warriors have also come to the party! More for me to kill! HA HA HA!!

That's when a door opens and flooding out of the door is the red realm archers. Now the fighting becomes vicious. The dust and sounds of death rise to the sky. Maubuus feels such joy at the chaos.

Hideo: Shazal I have an idea. Step put a step high in the air.

A step appears high above the fighting. Hideo opens a door and tells Shazal to go through. The door leads to the step in the air. Hideo and Calmar also go through the door and arrive at the step with Shazal.

Hideo: Warriors stop fighting!

Calmar: Scientists stop fighting!

Shazal: Archers stop fighting!

Maubuus' men listen to Shazal and stop fighting.

Maubuus: Shazal! You traitor!

Maubuus fires a laser gun at Shazal but it hits the force field that Maubuus has erected.

Shazal: Take the castle!!

The unified horde swarms the castle. The castle guard remain loyal to Maubuus. The numbers are too overwhelming though. The horde sweeps into the castle. Maubuus' last two wizards join him on the tower. A golden arrow screams through the air and kills Milstar's fellow wizard.

Maubuus: Get away from the edge!

Milstar: We're losing Maubuus. They're fighting their way through the castle.

Curos and Ag come running up the steps to Maubuus.

Curos: They're coming! We're trapped!

Sword, Arrow, and Calmar come out at the top of the tower.

Arrow: It's over Maubuus!

Maubuus: Not quite.

Curos jumps out of nowhere and begins fighting Arrow.

Sword: Maubuus, you're mine.

Maubuus: Haven't we done this before?

A swarm of birds swoop down and get in Sword's face. Maubuus pulls out the remote control to the door.

Maubuus: Goodbye all!

A rectangular door opens and Maubuus slips through it. Milstar and Ag jump in behind Maubuus. The door closes immediately.

Curos: Maubuus! Maubuus! Don't leave me!

Curos has devoted his entire life to Maubuus. Maubuus is the one person that Curos has respected. The one he has patterned himself after. The one person he admires.

The birds disperse from around Sword. Sword uses his Sword to impale Curos, who is being held by Arrow.

Curos: AAA!

Arrow: Maubuus' reign is finally over. It's OVER!!

Cheers resound throughout the castle. There is no more threat to the yellow realm.

Councilman 1: We've defeated Maubuus just two days before we were to be destroyed!

CHAPTER 15

BROKEN CHAINS

The yellow realm only has 1 great ocean. It's called the pink ocean because of the pink flies that swarm near its shore and sometimes alight on its surface. They create pink waves on the ocean. Their sunning of themselves is interrupted as Maubuus breaks to the surface of the ocean. Maubuus puts the entire door machine on his back and swims for shore. Milstar comes up and sees Maubuus.

Milstar: Maubuus! It's too far. I can't make it. Please help me.

Maubuus: Help yourself!

Ag is also in the water, he allows himself to float. The current carries him closer to the shore.

Milstar grabs the end of the door machine and pulls himself onto the machine. Maubuus doesn't care. His strong strokes take him closer and closer to the shore. He swims for hours until he finally reaches the shore. Maubuus throws the machine and Milstar off his back.

Maubuus' stare is the most evil thing ever created some of his enemies say. Today maybe it is.

Back at the warrior's city a spontaneous citywide celebration has broken out. The celebration lasts the rest of the day and begins again in the morning. The whole city is drinking and partying. Hideo has never seen Arrow drunk. This day is the first time. Arrow is so relaxed. He's smiling and happy. The people are dancing in the streets.

Calmar and the councilmen are still with the warriors.

Calmar: Warriors, I am please to call you my friends. Our people will forever be friends with yours. We may owe our very existence to you. By preemptively destroying Maubuus our civilization has been saved. But we will hold off on telling the people our dirty secret for a couple of days just in case!

Hideo: It sounds like a good decision.

Calmar: Arrow, you are a bold and good leader. I'm sure that as long as you lead there will always be prosperity. Hideo, you have a heart and an imagination that will never be matched. Arrow is the head but you are the heart of the warriors.

Hideo: Thank you Calmar.

Calmar: And Sadastra don't let yourself ever believe that you are inferior because you were created in a laboratory from Arrow's mother's blood.

Arrow: What?!

Hideo: Sadastra is a clone. She was made from the blood of your mother.

Arrow: Why wasn't I told?!

Hideo: We just found out. We were going to tell you.

Arrow: LIARS!! She is an abomination! She dishonors my mother's memory!!

Barrier: Calm down Arrow. This is a happy occasion.

Arrow: NO! My mother's blood was stolen!

The anger and raw emotion in Arrow's voice denotes the sacredness his people ascribe to the blood! It also exemplifies the hurt Arrow feels. -A hurt from childhood that was never truly expressed.

Sadastra begins to cry.

Hideo: Stop it, Arrow! She can't help that she was brought into the world this way.

Arrow: I don't care! Get her out of my sight before I kill her!

Sadastra: I'm sorry. I'm sorry!

Hideo: Don't apologize! You have a right to be alive!

Arrow: I've warned you! Get her away or I will kill her!

Hideo: If you touch her I'll ...

Arrow: You'll what?

Hideo: I'm LEAVING!!

Arrow: Go away! We don't need you!

Calmar: Calm down. Calm down!

Hideo flashes a door open.

Barrier: Think about what you've done!

Hideo holds Sadastra in his arms. Arrow begins to shine.

Hideo: Let's go!

Hideo pulls Sadastra along with him through the door to another part of the yellow realm.

On the shore of the Pink Ocean, Maubuus sulks.

Maubuus: Milstar, prepare to control the dragon!

Milstar: Please master no. I cannot control it. At the battle of the fire it killed almost all of the wizards. It wiped out a whole army!

Maubuus: Are you disobeying me?

Milstar: No sir.

Milstar begins to concentrate as Maubuus flicks on the door machine. The machine comes on emanating an eerie green light. Milstar begins to chant directly at the machine. First he begins slowly then he picks up the pace.

Maubuus impatiently waits, as nothing seems to be happening. Then Maubuus notices that the green light is gradually changing in hue. Now it's beginning to change hues faster. It's quickly cycling through the colors now. Then everything stops. The machine is still on because the sound it makes can still be heard. But there is no color emanating from the door. Milstar then stops. He gets up and walks into the door.

There are very tense moments as Maubuus waits. Growls and grunts come from the door and then the sound of Milstar barking orders. Next there are pleas. Then there are screams. Milstar is begging for his life. Milstar comes running out of the doorway.

Maubuus: Where is the Dragon?

Dragon: I AM HERE!!

The sound of its voice sends tremendous vibrations through the air. Maubuus laughs. The dragon comes fully out of the door. It is long and black with green white eyes. Its muscles ripple as it walks. And its scales glisten in the sun. Every step it takes leaves an impression upon the ground. But still there is a beauty to its movements.

Maubuus: Will you do what I say?

Dragon: NEVER!

Maubuus: Then we must fight.

Maubuus uses his laser gun. He hits the dragon in the leg. He doesn't want to kill it since he figures that he will need it. To Maubuus' surprise that laser does nothing to the dragon. Maubuus decides to shoot the dragon in the head. Again it does nothing to the dragon. The dragon smiles.

Dragon: Today is the day you die!

The dragon's tone is smug and evil. This is usually Maubuus' role.

Maubuus: I see that you wish to be stubborn.

Maubuus looks at the laser gun. He sees that it is set on its maximum setting. Maubuus runs to the dragon and jumps at its neck. Maubuus slashes his nails across the dragon's neck. The flesh of dragon's neck rips but it zips itself back together. It's like watching a zipper. Maubuus is impressed as he lands on the ground. Maubuus decides to make another slash but as he jumps, he is swatted down by the dragon's immense black paw. Maubuus is slammed to the ground. With all of the fighting, no one notices Ag's body wash up upon the shore.

Maubuus: Well, this is going to be fun.

Dragon: I agree.

Milstar looks on unable to help. He is still woozy. Milstar's magic has always focused on an affinity with birds. He has practiced so many hours of so many days of so many years! He's practiced so much that he naturally slips into his meditative state. He feels the birds all over the planet. He feels their thick wings as they flap. He feels the fresh air as they glide. He feels the dry bark on the tree limbs as the roost. He is a million birds at once. He sees millions of scenes flash before him until he sees one that holds his attention. It's a picture of Hideo and Sadastra. Hideo and Sadastra are standing on the beach of Center Island. Hideo has his hand around Sadastra's shoulder. They are quietly walking along the beach.

Hideo: Let's get some firewood and spend the night on the beach.

Sadastra: Ok ... Oh, Hideo ... I'm worried!

Hideo: After all the nasty things Arrow said to you, you are still worried about him. That's why I love you, Sadastra.

Sadastra: But what about the warrior's prophecy?

Hideo: Don't worry. There are no more threats to the warriors.

Sadastra: Maubuus wasn't found.

Hideo: Sadastra! Don't worry. I'll go back and transfer my powers to the kid that was supposed have them in the first place. Then they'll have their Doorway!

Sadastra: But it didn't work before.

Hideo: But before there were threats. They needed my way of thinking to contrast Arrow's. With no threats, the ancestors will have no reason to need me.

Sadastra: You think?

Hideo: Yes, I think. Sadastra, you worry about everything. Let's just enjoy a little time together.

Hideo and Sadastra pause for a moment and then they kiss.

They are lost in their love for each other. They never notice the circling seagull. Whose eyes are fixed on them. It's a seagull playing host to the senses of Milstar.

Milstar is broken out of his trance by Maubuus' body being slammed into him.

Maubuus: Get out of my way!

Maubuus and the dragon are so much alike. They are both cold and evil. The only difference is that the dragon has no dreams of world conquest. It just wishes to serve itself. It doesn't need anyone else. Maubuus needs the dragon hence the current conflict.

Milstar has never seen Maubuus fight so savagely. He has never seen the true strength that Maubuus can summon up. Maubuus actually lifts the entire dragon and throws it to the ground! He dodges the devastatingly powerful blows of the dragon. But there is no doubt that Maubuus cannot win this battle alone. Milstar again tries to join the battle. He concentrates on subduing the will of the dragon.

Dragon: NEVER AGAIN!!

The dragon swipes at Milstar but Milstar stops concentrating and just runs away. Nothing Maubuus does seems to harm the dragon in the least. The dragon actually seems to be somewhat holding back. It is somewhat in intrigued by Maubuus' ability.

Dragon: It is time for you to die.

The dragon lets out a flurry of vicious slashes that Maubuus does his best to avoid. The fight continues for hours until Maubuus is exhausted. Maubuus finally realizes that he will not win this fight.

Maubuus: Do you wish to yield?

Dragon: Why should I yield when I'm about to kill you?!

Maubuus: I will kill you mercifully if you yield.

Dragon: Who do you think you are?

Maubuus: I AM MAUBUUS!! Now come closer so that I may eat you!

Dragon: WHAT?! EAT ME?!! I WILL EAT YOU!!

The dragon springs its head forward and bites Maubuus in half!

Milstar stands stunned. The perfectly evil eyes of the dragon mesmerize him. He stands there studying them until he realizes that they are focused on him. Milstar slowly takes a step backward. The dragon doesn't move. Milstar's saucer shaped eyes plead as he takes another step backward. The pleas don't register on the dragon.

Then everything seems to move in slow motion. The dragon's large muscles clench then ripple into motion. Milstar tries to back up again as his magic seems to leave him.

The dragon roars as it moves. Its roar seems to freeze Milstar's blood. The dragon's monstrous head reaches Milstar. Milstar stares down its throat. Then suddenly the dragon's head falls to the ground. Milstar sees that the dragon isn't moving. But the only thing that Milstar can think of is escaping.

Milstar: What will I do now?

Milstar turns and walks away. As he's walking he hears movement by the dragon. Fear brushes over Milstar again. He decides to ignore the sound and keep walking. That's when he hears something that he cannot ignore. He hears the dragon speak.

Dragon: Milstar!

Milstar turns to see the dragon again raise its body. The voice of the dragon is different. It's the sound of...

Milstar: Maubuus?!

Dragon: Yes, this is Maubuus.

Milstar: But...

Dragon: But what? I now have the perfect body to exact my revenge. It is so strong, so deadly and yet ... it ... it feels like it somehow isn't here.

Milstar: What?

Dragon: I do not care! Tomorrow begins my revenge! First I will destroy the treacherous archers and then I will destroy those scientists! Next will be the warriors!

Milstar: Hideo is not with the warriors right now. He is alone with the girl again. The time is perfect to kill him.

Dragon: Ag, take this spit of mine. It is a virulent poison. Place it upon your boomerangs and go kill Hideo and Sadastra tonight!

Unseen to most, Ag comes out of hiding.

Ag: My pleasure.

On the island Hideo and Sadastra sit near a beautiful fire looking at the stars.

Hideo: I've always been a dreamer Sadastra. I've daydreamed about some of the craziest things. But I never dreamed anything like my current situation.

Sadastra answers in a jokingly shocked tone.

Sadastra: Oh, you never dreamed that you would be on an island in the middle of a distant realm, wielding the power of a doorway talking to genetically engineered alien?

Hideo: No, I meant that I never dreamed that I would find a woman as beautiful as you.

Hideo can see that Sadastra is taken by his words. They close their eyes and lean forward to meet in a kiss. Their lips do not meet. Hideo's chest meets Sadastra's hands as she pushes him away laughing.

Sadastra: It takes a little more to get a kiss out of me.

Sadastra stands.

Hideo: Like what?

Hideo stands.

Sadastra: Like ... you have to prove you can catch me!

Sadastra turns and runs. Hideo flashes open a door. Sadastra stops as the wind starts blowing.

Sadastra: No power!

Hideo closes the door and the wind dies down.

Hideo: I told you before I don't need my powers to catch you!

Sadastra: Oh? Then you don't mind giving me a head start.

She waves her hand and the wind blows Hideo down.

Hideo: Hey!

Hideo gets up and gives chase. He sees her run into the gently sloping hills but realizes that he's lost her. But then he hears her laughter. It comes from a cave that has an eerie pink light coming out of it. He runs into the cave and sees that it is lined with the glowing pink flies. They must sleep here.

Hideo runs on. He passes the opening to a large cavern. He stops momentarily to look in but he does not see Sadastra. Sadastra has to laugh because she's hiding near the large cavern's entrance and Hideo doesn't see her.

Hideo hears her though. So he turns to get her. She runs into the cavern only to see that there is no way out! She stamps her foot as Hideo enters smiling. She seems to slowly turn as Hideo anticipates holding her warm body. He sees her naughty smile as her head comes around and her hair falls from her face.

Then her face turns to horror as she sees something behind Hideo. It's Ag. Ag throws two-edged boomerangs in rapid succession. Hideo turns to see what has frightened Sadastra so much. He turns just in time to see a boomerang deflected from hitting him by Sadastra's wind. Ag quickly flicks a third boomerang, which is also laced with the dragon's poison saliva. With a reflexive thought Hideo opens two doors. -One into which the boomerang flies and one out of which the boomerang flies. The exiting door appears directly in front of Ag. The boomerang strikes Ag in the chest. Ag falls dead - immediately killed by the strange toxin.

Hideo: I got him!

Hideo turns to see Sadastra laying in a clump on the cavern floor.

Hideo: Sadastra? Sadastra!

Hideo sees that a boomerang has struck her in the stomach. He runs to her but he can do nothing except cry over her lifeless body. The tears stream from Hideo's face. He's never felt such pain.

Hideo: No, Sadastra! Sadastra! I love you, Sadastra!

His voice finally disturbs the pink flies, which begin a frenzied flight. A flight as frenzied as Hideo's emotions.

CHAPTER 16

THE REVENGE OF MAUBUUS

In the Yellow Realm the most advanced group here is known as just the scientists. There was a time when the leaders of the scientists were afraid that they would be wiped out. Now they are at complete peace with all the powers in the realm, they are still militarily superior to all the other cultures and Calmar is once again a councilman. There is a feeling of uneasy self-assurance this morning. Things seem to be all right. There have been no incidences of trouble this morning. But then it comes. A messenger runs into the council room.

Messenger: Sirs, I have grave news.

Calmar: What is it?

Messenger: The Archers have been decimated. They have been dispersed by a mighty creature.

Calmar: A mighty creature?

Messenger: Yes. It seems that this creature was a ... a dragon.

Calmar: A dragon? Enato, maybe we should call up the guard.

Enato: I agree. How do you say councilman?

Meer: I agree too. We need to get through this day.

Enato: Then a full alert it is.

Messenger: I shall sound the alert.

With the alert the scientists scurry back and forth. They all work quickly to prepare for an attack. A few minutes later the messenger returns.

Messenger: We are ready for attack. And sir, we are tracking a beast heading this way. We have sent the hoverships to intercept it before it reaches us.

Meer: Good idea.

A chill of fear goes through the council.

Enato: I guess we can't do anything but wait now.

Calmar: There is one more thing that we can do. We can ask for help from the warriors.

Enato: What can they do? Our weapons are more powerful than them. Besides we don't even know if this is a real threat.

Calmar: Maybe you're right. We'll wait a little longer.

Time goes by. Now it's around 10 a.m.

Messenger: All of the hoverships have been destroyed.

There is a state of disbelief that fills the room.

Enato: What kind of beast could destroy a hovership? Calmar, you hold sway with the warriors please go and summon them.

Calmar: I will. But I have no mode of transport. All the hoverships are destroyed and we don't have any working doorway machines.

Enato: It is a long walk but we will send some guards with you.

Calmar: I will return as soon as I can.

Calmar starts out on his long 2 hours walk. He doesn't realize that the dragon is nearly to his home.

When the dragon arrives. The scientists give him a fearsome welcome. Laser cannons blaze and the last guards move. The scientists are not militaristic and this was not a military expedition but still their weapons are impressive and their firepower is awesome. It is enough to give a light show for miles around. The brute force of the weapons pounds the dragon but still the dragon comes. The weapons seem to have no affect upon it. They do slow the dragon down. They make it harder for him to do his dirty work. Still he slashes buildings. He stamps on ordinary people. Maubuus the dragon is on a hateful rip.

Dragon: Feel the vengeance of Maubuus! I am the mightiest creature in this realm. I shall rule. You created me to rule all! I AM MAUBUUS!!

The sound of his mighty roars sometimes outdoes the sound of weapons! Maubuus' bragging is not heard by the warriors though. The warriors had noticed the spectacular light show happening so early in the morning. They became alarmed and are heading to the scientists abode to see what is happening.

Barrier: Look up ahead. Someone is coming.

Step: Maybe it's a guard from some of those downed hoverships that we passed.

Barrier: Did you see the condition of that ship? I don't think that anything could have survived that.

Sword: What could have done that? And why?

Arrow: Let's worry about the person approaching.

Arrow begins to shine and all the other warriors follow suit.

Sword: Hey, I think it's Calmar.

Arrow calls out to Calmar.

Calmar: Warriors! Please help me. My people are under attack.

Step: We could tell something was happening by all the fire in the sky. We came because we saw the fire created by your hoverships. But by the time we got to them they were destroyed. Then fire started coming from the direction of your city so we decided to come help.

Arrow: How many enemies are you facing?

Calmar: We think that there is but one.

Arrow: One? Only one destroyed all those hoverships?

Calmar: And the stronghold of the archers!

Barrier: This is a powerful enemy. But surely he cannot overwhelm all of your defenses.

Calmar: I dearly hope not.

The light show cannot be seen from Hideo's point but he is not looking up as he prays anyway. The tears have not stopped from him. He has spent the better part of the morning constructing a little wooden raft to bury Sadastra at sea since she is a woman without a land.

Hideo: Why! Why did you have to die Sadastra? You saved me and let yourself be hit. I should have died! I wish that I had died!

He continues to wish that he had died. He doesn't realize that in a way he has.

Back in the city of the scientists...

A newcomer has come to the city. A man that is actually already dead. His name is Koro. He's been sent on a mission from the past to see what happened to his people. It seems that he is late as he surveys the damage and walks around. He sees the many dead bodies and destroyed buildings. He reports his every movement as he goes along.

Suddenly, Koro hears screams to the northwest. He rushes to the screams. His blood is rushing and his heart pounding. He desperately hopes to save whoever is in need. For Koro is a very good man. He arrives and sees another dead woman. He hears more sounds from around a nearby building and decides to take a look.

He rounds the building and sees the newly arrived warriors. Hideo and the warriors were the prime suspects in the scientist's minds for destroying the city. So, Koro knows that he must report what he sees.

Koro: I see the warriors but I don't see Hideo!!

Those are the last words that Koro will ever say as he is struck down by the dirty claws of Maubuus the Dragon!

Calmar: Look over there! There's the dragon! It just killed another one of my people!

The two guards that Calmar had brought with him immediately open fire on the dragon.

Dragon: Can't you see how useless it is to fight me?

Arrow: That voice! It's Maubuus!!

The dragon's shape changes. It changes to that of Maubuus! The warriors look on in amazement.

Maubuus: How do I do it? I'm not sure. I just know that this body isn't quite here.

Sword: You're going to die Maubuus!! Once and for all!

Maubuus: Oh, are you angry because I killed your little lover girl Shatter. You didn't know that I ate her body and fed the scraps to the castle dogs!

Sword gets ready to charge Maubuus as anger just overwhelms him.

Arrow: Calm down Sword. This is his last day. He loves to entice.

Maubuus: I love to kill too. But then you know that since I killed your father.

Maubuus begins to laugh uncontrollably as all the warriors begin to shine.

Maubuus: Oh, I don't think you want to play with me. So, how about the dragon!

Maubuus' body changes to that of the dragon's again.

Five wolves of pure light charge the dragon. Arrow begins firing off arrows straight into the face of the dragon. The dragon tries to move its head out of the way but Arrow is far too accurate. Arrow hits every time.

The dragon breathes in to get ready to let out a mighty roar. When it does fire comes out of its mouth and nostrils.

The warriors scatter so none of them get hurt. Glass manages to get behind the dragon while Arrow, Sword and Step remain in the front. The dragon swipes and manages to catch one of Calmar's guards. The dragon squeezes the guard's body until it pops. At the same time Sword slices off the dragon's paw. -The paw that held the guard.

Dragon: AAA!

The wolves latch on to the extremities of the dragon and tenaciously chew and rip. The dragon takes its one free hand and swipes again. He swipes into the blue shield of Barrier. Finally something that dragon didn't slice through immediately.

The dragon slams its paw on the ground not realizing that Glass has slipped a large piece of glass under the dragon's foot.

There is a great explosion in which the warriors are blasted into all directions. But the dragon is too! The dragon doesn't move as the warriors recover.

Shiftblade: I guess we did it.

Barrier: It looks like it.

Arrow: Let's burn its body.

Sword and the last guard move over to the dragon. Its black carcass seems to stink of sulfur.

Sword: It's smell. It makes me dizzy. I can't think ... Arrow, what are we doing?

The guard seems visibly confused too.

Glass: What is this beast?

The dragon raises its head.

Dragon: I am Maubuus!

The dragon springs and uses BOTH of his claws to grab.

Glass: Where did the other claw come from?

Barrier: It's alive!!

Arrow: Warriors!

The dragon stuffs the guard down his throat. He then stuffs Sword into his mouth. Sword immediately Shines. As he goes down the dragon's throat, he slams his sword down the dragon's throat.

Sword: DIE!

Dragon: AAA!

The dragon gurgles as if choking. Sword falls to the ground. Touch runs over to Sword only to be slashed in half by the dragon.

Sword: Holy!

The sword in the dragon's throat disappears, just as an enormous arrow strikes the dragon in the chest. It knocks the dragon backward.

Dragon: That is the last straw!

Sword, Arrow, Glass, Step, Beast, and Shiftblade begin to retreat.

The dragon pops up and breathes fire onto Beast. Beast cries in agony as he is burned alive. Glass drops her red bomblets. These are explosive pieces of red glassy light.

The dragon basically ignores these as he continues to make his way to the warriors.

Dragon: Come on Arrow! Fight me! Avenge your father! I killed him!

Arrow stops and so do the rest of the warriors.

Shiftblade: We have to get out of here! It's too powerful.

Dragon: Come forth Arrow son of Bolt! Your father took my challenge! He wasn't a coward but he gave birth to one.

Arrow: I AM HERE! Let the rest of the warriors go and fight me.

Smiling, the dragon breathes and thin wisps of gray smoke stream from its nostrils.

Dragon: Of course.

The warriors watch as Arrow walks forward.

Glass: We can't let him fight by himself.

The dragon crouches ready to pounce. Anticipation can be seen in its cold green eyes.

The dragon springs. But he doesn't pounce on Arrow. He attacks the warriors that Arrow has left. It catches them by surprise and strikes Glass dead!

Arrow: NOOO!! NOOO!

The dragon slashes insanely. He also kills Sword and Shiftblade. Only Barrier survives.

Arrow: You liar!

Dragon: Doesn't it hurt to be helpless?

Arrow charges the dragon. The dragon simply grabs both Arrow and Barrier and takes to the air. Calmar watches from ground. He is forgotten by all. He wonders what will become of everything.

Later...

Arrow opens his eyes and sees that his hands are chained to the ceiling. He looks beside him and there is Barrier. His hands are also chained to the ceiling.

Arrow: Barrier. Barrier.

Barrier: Ugn ...

Arrow: Wake up.

Barrier: Where are we?

Arrow: It looks like ... I, Think we are in Maubuus' castle.

Into the room walks Bolt.

Arrow: What?!

Bolt: Son. I have to get you out of here.

Arrow: You're not my father. My father died.

Bolt: I didn't die. It was a lie. Maubuus kept me and tortured me for years.

Arrow: Then let me loose father.

Bolt starts laughing.

Bolt: You don't believe me. That's pretty funny.

He laughs maniacally as his body changes to that of Maubuus.

Maubuus: It's time for you to die.

Maubuus slashes off the warrior's head.

Maubuus: All the opposition is gone! I am the ruler of this realm. All I have to do is defeat the policing forces of the warrior's city.

Milstar has entered the room and has been listening.

Milstar: There is still one warrior left.

Milstar holds up a mirror. The mirror shows Hideo through a bird's eyes.

Maubuus stares.

Maubuus: The last one.

Hideo is sitting next to the river that runs through the middle of the island. The river winds down from hilly region in the center of the island to a small tree filled region and out to the ocean. It was this river he used to float Sadastra to the ocean. Hideo is sitting in a slightly inclined area a little distance from the patch of trees.

He's looking at the water imagining that he's dancing with Sadastra under a full moon. In his imagination everything is OK. He is so happy dancing. In his dreams the wind is cool and there are torches surrounding an open patio. It feels like they are one body attached by the music's airy vibrations.

He is brought out of the dream by a sound from his back. He turns and sees flames whiz past him –grazing his chest. Fear and surprise are interrupted by the pain of the bolt of fire. His sudden turn was the only thing that stopped the bolt from hitting him in the heart. As he falls backwards he sees Milstar standing atop a little hill.

Hideo falls toward the water in seemingly slow motion. He wonders about the end as he falls - as he instinctively opens a door to fall into, over the water. The door opens in the air over the beach and Hideo finds himself tumbling out of control toward the ground.

Hideo: AAA!

He opens a door horizontally to fall into and a door near the ground vertically to come out of. Hideo is seemingly spat out of the vertical door. He lands in the soft sand of the beach. The salt of the water stings the open sore caused by the fire bolt. Blood drips onto the sand as Hideo watches it in disbelief. Then he hears the voice of the one that has been responsible for so much of Hideo's trouble. -The voice responsible for ordering the death of Sadastra. -The voice of Maubuus. Hideo looks up with the hurt hatred flaming in his eyes. It's immediately replaced by fear.

Dragon: Hideo.

Hideo: Maubuus?

Dragon: Maubuus the dragon!

Hideo's fear shows.

Dragon: Where's Sadastra?!

Hideo feels a snap. He fills with uncontrollable anger. A seemingly thousand doors appear.

Dragon: Are you ready to die too?

Hideo: You will die Maubuus!

The doors swirl as Maubuus comes forward. Maubuus swipes his sooty claws at Hideo. Hideo immediately opens a door to block Maubuus' claws but the claws rip the door and nearly hit Hideo. Hideo doesn't have time to be stunned at what has just happened.

Hideo moves to open another door. He opens a door under the dragon. The dragon doesn't fall through though. It uses the back of its paw to slap Hideo down. Hideo struggles to get back to his feet. Everything is a bit blurry but Hideo knows that he must keep fighting or else he will surely die. Hideo opens a door for himself to move through but as he steps to it the dragon slashes it. Once the circle is broken he can't step through it. The dragon knows that. It slashes at the legs of Hideo. Hideo has practiced with the warriors for over half a year but he still isn't quick enough to fully escape the claws of the dragon.

Hideo: AAAAAAAA!!!!

Hideo falls to the ground again. He's writhing in bloody pain as the dragon moves over him. Hideo somehow gets his wits as the dragon sees the symbol of the warrior's people. It freezes, mesmerized by the hypnotic eye. The dragon strains to resist. Finally it snatches itself away. When it turns back Hideo is gone. Hideo hasn't gone far. He's so weak. He knows that he can't fight anymore. He sits beside a tree in the wooded patch of the island. Maubuus knows that Hideo hasn't gone far.

He can just feel him. Maubuus lets his sense of smell take him to the trees beside the river. There he sees an exhausted Hideo sitting beside a tree deliriously talking to himself.

Maubuus smells victory. He decides to make one final jab at Hideo's emotions. He lets his form become Sadastra.

Dragon/Sadastra: Oh Hideo! Hideo!

Hideo hears Sadastra's voice. He looks at her beautiful face. He remembers her tender touch and the bubbly joy in her laugh.

Hideo: Sadastra, I love you.

Sadastra runs to Hideo and hugs him. It feels like home. He's taken into the embrace of a dream. But still he wonders how. Sadastra lets go and looks lovingly at Hideo.

Dragon/Sadastra: Let me get you a drink of water. You sit and rest. I'll take care of your wounds.

Sadastra turns and goes to the river. She picks up a deep-cupped leaf. Hideo watches her. He notices that she is leaving a trail on the ground. A trail like there is a tail under her dress. But Hideo shakes it off as he enters his delirium again. The wheem sound seems a natural by-product.

Sadastra spits dragon's poison into the water with an evil smile. The smile turns sweet and innocent as she turns back to Hideo. She comes close to Hideo and holds out the leaf with the poisoned water in it.

Dragon/Sadastra: Here, drink this. You'll feel better.

Hideo doesn't say anything. He takes the leaf and drinks. He closes his eyes as he turns up the leaf. When he opens his eyes he sees Maubuus and Milstar standing there. Milstar hands Maubuus the remote control that he has retrieved from Ag's dead body. They both grin evilly. Everything is so confused as Hideo grabs his stomach and falls to his knees. Maubuus and Milstar turn away as a yellow rectangular door opens. Together Maubuus and Milstar walk away as Hideo falls face first into the dirt.

Maubuus and Milstar return to Maubuus' castle. Their next conquest will be the warrior's city.

Milstar: They always said that once the doorway leaves all the warriors will die.

Maubuus: I used to hate all the stupid beliefs that the warriors had. But now that one sounds so melody filled.

The two laugh.

Elsewhere...

Calmar looks at the last of his people's civilization and mourns. He sees the destroyed buildings and the dead bodies. He breathes the smoke that once was a mighty technological marvel. It was a scientific outpost that had become his home. It was so full of life but now it is full of death. Death brought on by their dreams of control. Their desire to control created an instrument which took control from them. Yes, there is death everywhere.

In his sadness he sits on the concrete of a wall. There he sees a stirring. There are still some people alive. With everything seemingly calm they are coming out. They are mainly women and children. Calmar is an old man. But he knows that these people will need help and leadership. He still has medical supplies in his cave. The situation is dire but it is a chance for an old man to do some good in his final years...

Later on the island...

Hideo's body remains motionless as the ghosts of the dead come to claim him. The ghosts of all the warriors he knew come to lead him to the world of the spirits. One particularly loving female spirit looks like

Sadastra. The ghosts stand there bewildered as Hideo begins to move. He is not dead. He opens his mouth and a doorway comes out. The doorway in which he poured the liquid that Maubuus gave him to drink.

Hideo is shaking in fear as his mind recounts what has happened. He wanted to be a hero but he ended up just fulfilling an ancient prophecy of death. He too almost died.

Hideo: It's time to get out of here. No more of this! Spirits or ancestors or whatever I failed. Do you hear me?! Let someone else help the warriors. Please, please no more.

There is a soft feeling like tear drops, as tiny balls of light slowly flow out of his body. The ghosts watch in horror as the doors go away. Their movements are expressive of their distress but Hideo cannot see them. Their screams are nothing but silence to Hideo. The impassioned pleas fade like the light of the doorways moving away in the twilight. The ghosts begin to disappear as they realize that they can't communicate with him. The doors are all gone except for one. -The blue door, which he put the dragon's liquid into. All the ghosts are too, except for one -the ghost. She puts her hand on Hideo's shoulder. Hideo doesn't feel her but a door opens and pictures flash in that door. The pictures are horrible. Each picture is a picture of Sadastra or one of the warriors dying. -Pictures of the warriors dying at the hands of Maubuus. The pictures mesmerize Hideo. He sits watching them in disbelief.

Hideo: Everyone?

The pictures continue to flash with the gentle touch. The other ghosts also come back and watch.

Hideo: I can't just run away. I have to do something...or I'll be haunted forever. All of my friends are dead. Also the woman I love is too. I will do something.

Tears again flood out of his eyes as the light of the doors gently float back into him. The spirits look on and they smile. They feel the life in Hideo.

Hideo: What can I do? What can I do? There is no one to help me.

Hideo realizes that the first thing that he has to do is rest. The dragon knocked him around pretty badly. His sleep is troubled though. Troubled by the thoughts of being alone and not knowing what to do. Even when he enters the world of dreams he finds himself standing beside a river asking himself questions.

Hideo: What can I do? All the warriors together couldn't defeat Maubuus! What can I do? I am alone.

A voice answers.

Old Doorway: No. That isn't true. I am here.

Hideo: What?!

Old Doorway: Hideo, I have something to show you. I have to tell you what happened at the battle of the fire.

The early morning hours are a time of havoc for the city of the warriors. Maubuus the dragon has attacked! He quickly mopped up the little police forces of the city and commenced to just destroying and killing for sheer fun. He wantonly destroys everything he slashes.

Dragon: Who can stand up to me? Who can fight me?

The last priest of the city comes out to face Maubuus. Maubuus laughs with sheer elation that this little man is going to be able to do anything.

Priest: Maubuus! You must stop murdering these innocent people.

Dragon: Are you going to stop me priest?

Priest: I'm going to try!

Dragon: And what is it that you're going to do?

Priest: I'm going to surrender.

Maubuus is taken aback by the priest's words. Of course, Maubuus knew that he would win but he just never truly imagined ruling this city. He knows that the priest speaks for the city so he knows that he has won. He is the ruler of the yellow realm.

Maubuus: Organize a grand celebration in my honor. You, little priest, will prepare a crown for my head and a throne for me to sit upon. Do you understand?

Priest: I do.

Maubuus: This celebration will take place at noon today.

Priest: How can I do that? The sick and dying need my help. How can you have a celebration in the midst of such suffering?

Maubuus: Because I am Maubuus. Again, the celebration will take place at noon today. At this celebration you will crown me as the king of this city and the king of this realm.

In the world of dreams...

Hideo: Doorway, where are we going?

Old Doorway: Here. Look over there.

A chill of fear comes over Hideo as he realizes that this is the cave of the dragon he made up.

Old Doorway: Let's go inside.

Hideo: No we can't! There's a dragon in there.

Old Doorway: Come.

Hideo is very apprehensive but he follows Old Doorway into the cave. To his surprise there is no dragon in the cave.

Hideo: There's no dragon here. I wish that I could see better in here.

Suddenly Hideo notices that the cave has become brighter. In the light he sees a huge set of broken chains.

Hideo: At the power transfer ceremony, I was shown broken chains. I didn't understand. This is the dragon that is now Maubuus.

Old Doorway: I came to you because I felt that the dragon was connected to you.

The events they speak of start to enact themselves around them. It's like they're in a virtual reality setting.

Old Doorway: At the battle we waited for Maubuus' attack force. He sent some of his best-trained men with a lead squad of archers. Some of his wizards also came. Out of the sky came the dragon with a lightning fast strike. The dragon may have come out of a door. It immediately breathed a seeming ocean of fire. On the back of the dragon there were many of Maubuus' soldiers. So, they seemed to come out of nowhere. They were suddenly all around us fighting. I was the main target of the attack. I was hit hard and quickly. That's when the rest of Maubuus' men joined the fight. The dragon struck me. He struck me so hard doorways spewed out everywhere. They mixed with the smoke and fire, which also was everywhere. I got through a blue door before the dragon could kill me. When I saw you...

Hideo: You knew that I was somehow tied to the dragon. Then you gave me the power and went to the red... no...this realm!

Old Doorway: YES!!! The invisible doorway!

Hideo: After a little while a rectangular shaped door opened and a dragon came through. It was too much for Maubuus' wizards to control. The dragon slaughtered most of Maubuus' men along with the warriors.

Old Doorway: Yes! The wizards tried to return the dragon here! The dragon was beating most of them here too. The survivors escaped through the door and headed back to Maubuus.

Hideo: The dragon saw us and attacked! I turned and ran. You followed me. We ran into this cave. The dragon followed...

Old Doorway: Yes. I knew that you were responsible for the dragon and that you were responsible for this place. I reminded you of that! I reminded you that in the vast realm of imagination this was your spot.

Hideo: Then I came up with the plan to save our lives with magic chains. Chains that were strong enough to hold even this monster.

Old Doorway: The dragon entered the cave and you imagined chains growing out of the ground like vines! The chains wrapped around the dragon. It couldn't break the chains.

Hideo: The plan was perfect but the dragon's head was still free. It head butted you in the back into me. -Its sweat flying onto both of us. When you touched me you activated a door again. Again you chose a red door. This time we actually made it to the red realm.

Old Doorway: Not quite, Hideo. I died here. My body fell with yours through the red door. I died here in your imagination though. So, my spirit is here. I have a special connection to the place you created and to you.

Hideo: I understand. But two things I don't understand. The dragon IS Maubuus. He wasn't before. In fact, he wasn't even on Maubuus' side! What happened?

Old Doorway: I don't know what has happened. What's the other thing?

Hideo: Why couldn't I remember what happened?

Old Doorway: What are the powers of the dragon?

Hideo: I don't know.

Old Doorway: You do. You gave them to the dragon.

Hideo: I always thought of it as very powerful. It had claws that ripped reality, a breath of fire, and sweat that was a pox to the mind.

Old Doorway: It must've affected your memory as it did mine before death.

Hideo: So, what do we do?

CHAPTER 17

HEART OF THE WARRIORS

High Noon...

In the midst of terrible destruction a celebration is going on. The celebration is without heart. The entire city is there. No one is happy but everyone is cheering for the one about to be crowned king. Abruptly there is silence. The priest has come up to speak.

Priest: I come before you today to crown our new king. King Maubuus!

Maubuus stands as the crowd cheers. The priest holds a crown. He approaches Maubuus. Then he throws the crown to the ground.

Priest: I can't do this. This is an insult to all our ancestors.

Maubuus: Crown me or die!

Priest: I shall stand. I shall stand for what is right!

Maubuus: Then you will die!

Priest: Ancestors help me!

Maubuus reaches out for the priest but then seemingly disappears. He falls straight downward. The crowd is awed.

Priest: Thank you!

The priest gives his thanks to the ancestors but it is not them responsible for this. It was a young man in the crowd named Hideo. Maubuus has fallen through a colorless door –an invisible door. Hideo follows Maubuus into the realm of imagination.

Maubuus: What is this?! Who dares?! This place…I know this place. It is the home of the dragon.

Hideo: Yes it is. It is the realm of imagination. And I rule here!

Chains grow out of the ground bounding the dragon. Maubuus laughs.

Maubuus: You think you rule here but I can imagine too!

The chains turn to dust.

Maubuus: Hideo, you are a foolish boy!

The dragon slashes but a barrier appears. Frustration is easily read on the dragon's face. The dragon then smashes the barrier but Hideo has already moved. This type of battling goes on for about 20 minutes. Hideo is starting too worry because he realizes that if he makes a wrong move he'll be killed.

Maubuus is becoming really irritated. His new body doesn't get tired but the personality of Maubuus does. He realizes that he will have to use his wits to win.

Dragon: You have never been able to beat me Hideo. We've met here many times. You've been afraid to even enter my cave.

Hideo: Well this is now. There is always a first time.

As they talk, the titanic battle continues. Hideo strikes with a sword. The dragon blocks with a shield. The dragon breathes fire. Hideo counters with a flood of water.

Hideo didn't expect this. He figured that he could create in this realm but he didn't think that the dragon could. The dragon couldn't before. But now the dragon is Maubuus and Maubuus can imagine.

Dragon: Aren't you afraid Hideo? You know you can't beat me. You never could.

Hideo doesn't answer as desperation and self-doubt start creeping in.

Dragon: What was the prophecy Hideo? If you left the warriors then all the warriors would die. Well Hideo, you are the last one. You can't fight fate! All the warriors must die!

Hideo knows that the dragon is right as he falls down and the dragon pounces over him. He moves his face close to Hideo.

Dragon: All the warriors will die!

The dragon opens its large mouth and bites down on Hideo's head. Again time seems to move in slow motion. Hideo's whole life flashes before his eyes. He sees the good times and bad times of his childhood. He sees the earlier times with his parents and realizes/ feels how much they love him. He sees himself retreating to imagination when things wouldn't go right. Next he sees himself creating the dragon. And finally he sees his time with the warriors. Their faces flash saying many things. The last is Arrow.

Arrow: Warrior? You are NOT a warrior! You are a Doorway!

Hideo: I am not a warrior. And dragon, you are mist.

The dragon's teeth turn to mist as they contact Hideo's face.

Hideo: My imagination controls your body!

Dreams Unseen

Hideo opens a door as only Maubuus' spirit remains.

Maubuus: What?!

Old Doorway: Now you are mine!

Old Doorway's spirit pushes Maubuus' spirit out the door. Both are free to roam the world of the dead...

Dragon: Let me flow out the door too.

Hideo: What?!

Dragon: Almost every day you came here. You dreamed. You dreamed of being great. You dreamed of being a hero. And you dreamed of me. I saw! I saw your dreams! Then one day somehow I dreamed back! But my dreams were... **DREAMS UNSEEN!**

Hideo: What did you dream?

Dragon: I dreamed of freedom.

Hideo: Then go. You are only mist. You cannot hurt anyone.

There seems to be such great joy as the dragon flows through the door and mixes with the air. Wherever the wind could blow he could go. The dragon was free and Hideo was too.

A couple days later in the warrior city...

The wind is slightly cool and a hint of drizzle is in the air. The dampness stings Hideo's eyes like tears. Like the tears you never see heroes shed. Hideo had always wanted to be a hero. He had always wanted to feel the greatness of a hero. Now he feels the pain that comes along with being one. -The pain that is not spoken of in the legends and the comic books. He wonders to himself if the gratitude of a whole world can fill the emptiness left by the loss of a loved one.

Hideo stands in the position prepared for Maubuus. Having successfully transferred the doorway power to Ramethi yesterday, he is saying his farewell to the people. To his right stands the priest and to his left stands Calmar.

Hideo: It is finally time for me to leave you. Your future is now bright. Maubuus is gone. And all the peoples of this realm are united in peace and cooperation. There is a respect for the ancestors and traditions of the past but there is an openness to new ideas. Now I must go fix this in my life and create the brightness that I see here.

The crowd cheers as Hideo shakes hands with Calmar and the priest. And as they shake hands with each other, Hideo turns and silently walks through a waiting blue door.

THE END